chak
⊠ *a begi*

CW00959364

CHRIS STORMER

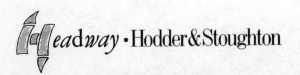
Headway • Hodder&Stoughton

This book is dedicated to my wonderful parents
Dick and Daphne Corner

Order queries: please contact Bookpoint Ltd, 39 Milton Park, Abingdon, Oxon OX14 4TD. Telephone: (44) 01235 400414, Fax: (44) 01235 400454. Lines are open from 9.00–6.00, Monday to Saturday, with a 24 hour message answering service. Email address: orders@bookpoint.co.uk

British Library Cataloguing in Publication Data
A catalogue record for this title is available from The British Library

ISBN 0 340 70472 1

First published 1998
Impression number 10 9 8 7 6 5 4 3 2 1
Year   2003 2002 2001 2000 1999 1998

Typeset by Transet Limited, Coventry, England.
Printed in Great Britain for Hodder & Stoughton Educational, a division of Hodder Headline plc, 338 Euston Road, London NW1 3BH by Cox and Wyman Limited, Reading, Berks.

CONTENTS

ACKNOWLEDGEMENTS

I had no hesitation in accepting, when asked to write this book. Having done so, however, I suddenly doubted whether channelling could in fact be 'taught'. My four previous books had been channelled through so intuitively that I had given no thought to the process itself. As soon as I began channelling, however, it seemed that the flow would never stop! Bringing through the contents of this book has been extremely enriching especially when, due to my hectic worldwide schedule, my parents stepped in to assist with the editing. My father's reaction was that this is exactly how he had always thought, but had never been able to put into words. This helped me to understand him and the frustration that he, like many others, had so often encountered. I am truly blessed to have such amazing parents and thank them for the many hours they dedicated to this book. Also my sincere appreciation goes to all my loving family, friends and colleagues. My beloved man, John Fryer and two gorgeous teenage sons, Andrew and David, provided, as always, endless support, plenty of space and abundant affection for which I am most grateful. Elizabeth Ann Rudd, my secretary, Veronica Polo-Polo, my housekeeper, Richard, my gardener, and Val Seddon, my other 'mother' have also been outstanding. My thanks also to Lesley Grobb who helped me 'lose' pages and fine-tune the manuscript. However, it is due to the foresight and faith of my editors Lucy Purkis and Sue Hart at Hodder and Stoughton that this book was conceived in the first place. None of this would have been possible without our celestial friends who continue to entrust us with phenomenal Universal wisdom. There are many times that angelic wings swooped in to make time and space available. With so many souls needing to be acknowledged, as well as those reading these words now, I thank you all.

ABOUT THE AUTHOR

Chris Stormer SRN, SCM, HV, Dip.R.

Chris has been channelling ancient wisdom regarding natural healing for over ten years and today is a recognised world authority on the subject. She is the author of four books on Reflexology, all of which have been published by Hodder and Stoughton, UK.

> *Reflexology* – Headway Lifeguides
> *Reflexology – The Definitive Guide*
> *Language of the Feet*
> *Teach Yourself Reflexology*

Reflexology is the ancient, gentle and sensitive massage and stimulation of specific reflexes of the body that are reflected in miniature on to the soles of the feet. This marvellous way of naturally balancing and harmonising all aspects (mind, body and soul) is exceptionally useful when reconnecting with the art of channelling.

INTRODUCTION

Every day, in countless ways, ideas, activities and resources emanating from a source that is far beyond human consciousness have a profound and indelible impact on life and the surrounding atmosphere. These are generally believed to be due to fate or Divine inspiration and may manifest in various forms of writing, painting, speech, music, routine activity, community work or even in a smile.

Everyone instinctively channels through day dreaming, prayer, meditation and so on, but only a few are consciously aware of this extraordinary gift. The world of channelling is so rich and varied it can be likened to going to an information centre to select data, or surveying a map to determine the best and most meaningful route. Either way, the journey through life becomes smoother and more significant.

Better still, the procedure requires no effort and no expenditure since it is merely an extension of thought processes which automatically link individuals with the enriching and abundant source of Universal wisdom. Those who have discovered the knack of channelling are amazed at its simplicity and are delighted to discover an effective tool that helps overcome stress, anxiety and extreme apprehension. They become increasingly aware of the effects and consequences of every perception, word, emotion and deed and use their knowledge advantageously to improve personal and general circumstances. In so doing, atmospheric states and environmental conditions can be altered beneficially, ultimately leading to a more worthwhile existence on earth.

Everyone has a unique and specific role in life, no one person being lesser or greater, yet we all reflect the lesser or greater parts of one

1

another. With Universal guidance, anything imaginable becomes possible and Divine assistance is always available on request. Situations, no matter how demanding or perceivably traumatic, can be viewed as being ideal and essential for personal growth and development.

This book shares various ways in which to channel and conveys archaic wisdom to ease and enhance the process. Exercises re-acquaint readers with innate talents that may have been forgotten, while practical guidelines allow the effectiveness of this powerful approach to be experienced enabling a more wholesome reality to be enjoyed. Select the most appropriate and enjoyable techniques, then expand and adapt these activities to suit your personal needs until channelling becomes a way of life. The intensity of feelings evoked will vary considerably, with the greatest reaction being towards those issues that need addressing the most. Decide for yourself whether you are ready to deal with any specific topic, or would prefer to return to the relevant section another time. If you are a sceptic, keep an open mind, as you discover more about the exciting and enriching world of channelling.

The process of channelling

What is channelling?

Through channelling energy is transmitted from one source to another with the way in which it is conveyed, received and utilised determining the eventual outcome. For example, if water lands on barren ground it has little or no effect but if it falls on fertile ground there can be abundant growth. Ultimately, through germination, new beginnings can be distributed. Everyone is a natural channel with the mind channelling thoughts, the body channelling actions and the soul channelling the spirit. An active channel shapes Universal information into transmutable, comprehensible forms and presents them to others to ensure the spread and utilisation of Divine wisdom for the survival and progress of humanity. The most wonderful aspect of channelling is that everyone already knows how to do it. All that is required to become a creative and effective source is re-acquaintance with the process. After this, the many exciting dimensions of the Universe become instantaneously accessible, enabling the mind to expand beyond the more mundane and monotonous aspects of life into a much wider perspective of the whole.

Why is channelling so important?

The earth is at a critical point in its development, with major shifts in values, lifestyles and spiritual orientation. Ongoing changes will cause the crumbling of outdated institutions and age-old structures

that belong to an earlier period of social development. This is the end of a phase, not the end of the world, and marks the beginning of an exciting new era of enlightened living. During this transitory period massive and powerful Universal energy shifts are transforming vibrational frequencies at atomic level. Channelling eases the change, as linear time and current concepts of reality are relinquished to make way for the next dimension of human existence.

how do these changes affect human beings?

Adjustments within the physical body can cause mood extremes, confused thoughts, heavy or chaotic emotions, extreme concern, excessive fear and self-doubt. It becomes more difficult to achieve results efficiently and effectively, leading to frustration and anger. Disturbed sleep patterns, restlessness, altered food preferences, clumsiness, minor 'accidents' and other inexplicable phenomena consequently may be experienced. Atoms take on an energy form and react to emotions to become 'events', rather than 'things'. A similar 'atom-event' reaction is created through channelling to allow a change of consciousness to occur.

what is the overall effect?

Planet Earth is so plagued by destruction, disturbance and disease from the greed, artificiality and uneasiness of humans, that only Divine intervention can provide solutions. Both mind and matter originate from the one Universal source and, being inseparable, form an indivisible channel of energy that links the whole of creation. Everyone and everything is an extension of the Creator's spirit and what happens to one part touches us all. Universal Guidance attained through channelling helps release the overwhelming sense of fear and insecurities that occurs from a perceived lack of control of earthly circumstances. Channelling re-directs the energy and creates completely new perspectives which re-establish balance and empower the individual. As body, mind and soul naturally become

attuned to greater states of awareness they learn to adapt with ease to the transformations that are taking place and can then cope with being catapulted into a stimulating new existence.

ARE THERE MANY WAYS TO CHANNEL?

There are as many different ways to channel as there are individuals, with everyone having their own specific method of effectively bringing through Universal wisdom. Channelling links everyone to the one Divine source, but within this energy are many dimensions or entities that are a part of it. Several of these aspects can be channelled simultaneously, although initially only one invisible friend is usually selected until confidence is gained. For instance, television is a channelling medium that can relay a tremendous variety of data to billions of people, although a single programme is selected at any one time.

Distribution of data via satellite and television

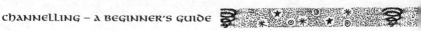

Just as the viewer can decide to use, convey, alter, expand or ignore the data received, so it is with channelling.

WHAT IS THE ORIGINAL SOURCE?

An eternal range of all knowledge is contained within the vast Hall of Ancient Wisdom, which is a massive Universal library that can be accessed at any time to extend perceptions and comprehension to a phenomenal extent. A wealth of guidance can be obtained from this spiritual source in the same way that advice and opinions are traditionally sought from other humans.

WHAT EVIDENCE IS THERE THAT CHANNELLING EXISTS?

Scientific research relies on analysing physically determined data, while the more intangible and extraneous aspects of life, such as channelling, are often dismissed due to a lack of irrefutable evidence. There is, however, no scientific proof of Divine existence in the form of God or any other deity, yet belief in this presence is strongly reinforced world wide through religious institutions and establishments. Channelling is the link with this source and once its powers have been experienced, there is little doubt about its actual effect.

HOW CAN THE DECISION TO CHANNEL BE MADE?

Develop the skill of channelling, explore its many facets and then determine the importance of the information before making a decision to channel. There are no harmful side effects since you are in the safe hands of the Universe. Initial uncertainty whether channelling is a fabrication of the mind, an unexplored function of the imagination or true communication with Universal beings is natural as it is all this and more.

BACKGROUND TO CHANNELLING

WHAT ARE THE ORIGINS?

Throughout history ideas, inventions and discoveries have been channelled through, as a source of prophecy, for society to develop and to cope with phenomenal changes on Earth. Since time immemorial there has been healing through contact with the spirit world. Around 5000 BC, the Egyptian 'Book of the Dead' contained descriptions of how the human soul leaves its physical body to communicate with the spirits of the deceased. Later, in Ancient Greece, oracles related messages from the Gods whilst in deep trances. The Old Testament mentions that Saul spoke 'in tongues' on the road to Damascus whilst the New Testament refers to Jesus as a channel for God. Despite the Christian Church discouraging channelling in the Middle Ages, the Shamans continued to induce dreamlike hypnotic states through fasting, dancing, chanting and even 'drugs' to merge with animal spirits and discover more about animal skills. One of the more recent channels is Edgar Cayce who channelled through over 9,000 life healings and medical readings and discovered that the Bible's Book of Revelation can be psychically interpreted.

WHAT BELIEFS SURROUND CHANNELLING?

Channelling was once believed to belong to a few elite and chosen souls but today everyone has the right and capacity to access psychically and connect intuitively with Universal wisdom. Each and every moment embraces a new opportunity for personal and overall advancement and development.

3 THE PRESENCE OF GUIDING FORCES

What is a guiding force?

The intuition, or sixth sense, is the Guardian Angel within everyone that protects, guides and inspires through awareness of intense feelings and overwhelming desires. It is a facet of the Higher Self, which resides in the Super Conscious mind as an integral part of the Universal mind and becomes more active when the mind is an open channel of awareness and whilst asleep.

What is a spirit guide?

Spirit guides are invisible friends that assist mortal souls to achieve their purpose on earth by mediating between individuals and the Creator. They do not seek recognition or need to have their existence proven, preferring that the focus of concentration be on the information and wisdom shared.

Why is spiritual guidance particularly important now?

Transition into new ways of thinking and behaving is so much easier with spiritual guidance and reassurance. Forming an association with a guide is like making friends with another soul on earth for mutual expansion and greater understanding of one another. Many invisible friends can be chosen just as one guide can befriend many channels.

EXERCISE TO OBTAIN GUIDANCE AND ASSISTANCE

A guide waits to be invited through prayer or meditation. Otherwise try the following fun and rewarding process.

- Write a specific invitation 'To whom it may concern' followed by 'Your assistance and guidance would be greatly appreciated'. Continue by stating personal attributes that you particularly wish to enhance such as: a sense of humour, innate wisdom, intuitive awareness and highlight areas of concern within these. Then ask for the faith and courage to apply the direction given and finish with a note of gratitude plus your signature.
- Read the words out loud several times, before throwing away or burning the invitation then wait for a response, which will come unexpectedly in beneficial ways. A note of acknowledgement is always appreciated. Invitations, requests and notes of gratitude can be dispatched daily, monthly or as often as necessary, until it eventually becomes a conscious way of life.

ARE THERE ANY DETRIMENTAL ASPECTS?

Everything in life is good or bad depending on how it is perceived. Traumatic experiences can either be a time of self-pity and destruction or an opportunity to discover inner strength and resourcefulness. The fear that an undesirable spirit may take over the mind, body and soul can be easily dissipated with the knowledge that the most appropriate guide is magnetically attracted to satisfy personal needs.

THE ROLE OF MEDIUMS

What is a medium?

The term 'medium' refers to a person possessed with the spirit. However, everyone is a medium with the only difference being that conscious mediums receive unseen messages and know how to shape them into intelligible forms before conveying the Universal wisdom to others.

These messages may, in turn, be relayed in part or fully through a further link or medium.

What is 'meaningless' information?

TV and radio transmissions may, for instance, appear meaningless, if they are in a foreign language or dialect. However, this does not mean that they are incomprehensible to everyone. The same goes for channelled information, the significance of which becomes clearer in time.

Do all mediums go into trances?

Some mediums choose to go into controlled trances to communicate, or to be a channel for spirits. In very deep trances, the medium leaves consciousness, vacates their physical body and allows a spirit, such as Lazarus, a well-known channelled entity, to take over. Inspired speeches made in this detached state are only one aspect of being a medium since the process itself simply involves connecting with a transpersonal level of the mind, which can be attained without going into a trance.

RECONNECTING WITH THE PROCESS

What is effective channelling?

To channel effectively, all personal thoughts and conditioned belief systems are put to one side for the mind to expand beyond the boundaries of conscious awareness. This is easier in the blissful state of alpha consciousness, induced through massage, reflexology or deep meditation, since complete relaxation of the body, mind and soul makes the whole being more receptive to Universal energies.

Exercise to enhance effective channelling

- **Appreciate the gift of life**. Bring to mind, or write down, everything that makes life worthwhile: physically, intellectually, emotionally and spiritually. Decide how to develop these concepts to make life an even more enriching experience.
- **Enjoy individual attributes**. Consider how your qualities, ideas and mannerisms make a difference and then write down your dreams and ambitions that still need to be realised, doing something each day towards making these come true.
- **Acknowledge unique skills**. Reflect on everything that you can do including the most basic skills, such as walking, talking, singing, and so on. Think of the pleasure derived and consider ways in which these assets could be enhanced.
- **Be natural and spontaneous**. Laugh when happy, cry when sad, hum for consolation. Smile frequently with genuine warmth,

especially to strangers, each of whom represents the 'stranger part' of us that we still need to know.

- **Openly and honestly express the true self.** Be yourself and be proud of who and what you are.
- **Remove all limitations.** Replace 'I can't' with 'I can'.
- **Develop healing abilities.** Warmly acknowledge and appreciate others.
- **Be self-assured.** Fill your being with renewed energy and enthusiasm.
- **Look for the good in everyone.** Take an interest in the wellbeing of others.
- **Enjoy the unexpected.** Life is full of surprises and unplanned opportunities for personal growth and development.

What does the process entail?

Channelling involves bringing non-physical, spiritual energies into the terrestrial realm. There are seven phases.

1 **Conception.** Recall non-physical experiences, such as an imaginary friend during childhood, seeing unusual *'déjà vu'* apparitions or having a near-death experience.
2 **Preparation.** Be ready to accept non-physical energies through deep relaxation, meditation and visualisation.
3 **Gestation.** Tune into the physical energies of the body and send soothing, loving thoughts to areas of tension or discomfort noting the effect of non-physical thoughts and emotions.
4 **Recognition.** Give the vibrancy a name such as Essence, Spirit of Life, Supreme Form, Universal Inspiration or whatever comes to mind.
5 **Implementation.** Consciously choose to become a channel and invite Universal guidance and assistance at all times.
6 **Integration.** Develop a trusting relationship between the earthly and spiritual energies for the Universal material to be used enthusiastically, beneficially and lucratively through teaching, counselling, painting, writing, healing, and so on.
7 **Maturation.** The total integration of energies for self-actualisation.

Is it safe to channel?

The only occupational hazard of channelling is self-doubt. Unusual experiences are most unlikely, unless desired. Take comfort from the fact that channelling is in two parts, each of which is contrary to one another. The first is a fixed point, based on the ideal, whilst the other is a free-flowing process, which is spontaneous and involves a willingness to let go. The stable base reassures the soul and gives it the confidence to liberally explore the metaphysical world. Once an ideal has been established the rest of the process follows naturally, with higher ideals creating greater security and complete liberation.

What can be expected from channelling?

Although everyone's experience of channelling is different it is always ideal for the person concerned. Children and teenagers sometimes have more 'way out' experiences due to their spontaneous, uninhibited and intuitive natures whereas adults often need greater reassurance. Channelled material expands the mind in ways that may be incomprehensible to others, resulting in many visionary concepts which are first rejected, then ridiculed but eventually, once put to the test, accepted. These stages allow society to slowly adapt to new ideas, especially when the change is drastic. Patience and the willingness to share Universal wisdom, regardless of perceived adversity ultimately become a worthwhile experience.

The channelling procedure itself

How can channelling be facilitated?

The main prerequisite for channelling is a profound curiosity and a genuine need to know. Owing to the diversity of individuals, there is

no one fixed method of approach or set formal procedure since expanded consciousness is reached in many different ways. It is best, therefore, to allow the most natural technique to intuitively unfold with assistance from the Universe. The ultimate form of channelling is simply to be the vessel for each individual spirit to channel itself through in its own unique physical form. The channelling ability can then intuitively return.

Is it possible to remain in control when channelling?

Although total abandonment of the conscious self and complete trust in the Divine are required to channel freely, the free will remains intact to prevent anything from possessing us against that will. The inherent ability to choose means that absolute control can be regained at any time. The link between the super conscious and the conscious ensures symmetry between the intellect and the intuition, providing greater control when channelling than at any other time.

What happens whilst channelling?

During channelling, the mind becomes temporarily detached from the outer terrestrial world and the five physical senses tune into finer internal frequencies that are connected to the resources of the Universe. In this altered state of awareness, visions may be seen, voices heard, new sensations felt and a wealth of information obtained whilst still conscious of environmental conditions. The nature of Universal wisdom and guidance is determined by personal development and the willingness to share it, whilst the depth of the trance-like state depends upon personal preference and the degree of attachment to consciousness. It is not, however, always essential to go into a trance. Channelling is just as effective, sometimes more so, when performing daily chores and other activities since unusual concepts can just as easily be triggered when walking, dancing or conversing. The flow of ideas is invariably encouraged by music, visual art and other forms of creativity.

14

How can I be sure that I am channelling?

Universal guidance produces an inner sense of pure knowing that is totally separate from any common sensory experience. As questions form, tentative solutions intuitively come to mind to be examined, rejected, refined or accepted. Receiving Universal guidance is like creative problem solving with awareness occurring as the solutions are applied. Exciting as this is, the greatest challenge is finding the time to integrate the vast amount of channelled material that is available.

Can energies be channelled in other ways?

Tuning into an object, such as a photograph can provide valuable information since it represents the reduced image of the greater energy pattern. This form of channelling is called 'psychometric'. It is based on the principle that everything, including inanimate substances such as stones, buildings and furniture carry their own electromagnetic vibrations, to reveal the unique qualities of their owners. Learning to resonate to nature and inanimate objects helps to bring everything to life intuitive and increases awareness. For complete understanding of the true self, being appreciative and respectful of the wonders of the world is an essential part of channelling.

How should channelled information be recorded?

The amount and content of material can be so overwhelming that it is not always possible to recall all the information. It is therefore advisable to keep a journal, carry writing materials at all times and categorise and store all information in a data storage system until an

outlet is found through counselling, teaching, writing, art, music and so on. Remember to always acknowledge the Divine source.

The benefits of Universal channelling

What are the advantages of effective channelling?

Enormous gratification can be gained from channelling Universal information since the mind wanders in multifarious directions and returns from the more subtle dimensions of Creation with a wealth of innovative information, perceptions and energies that bring ongoing enlightenment for human advancement and general wellbeing.

- Life is transformed through a redefinition of direction.
- Superficial appearances no longer conceal the beauty of the true essence.
- The soul's purpose is understood and appreciated.
- Greater insight is attained through complete trust of intuition.
- Connection with the true self generates a more creative and rewarding reality.
- Energy fields are energised, rejuvenated and restored on all levels.
- Mobility between different levels of consciousness brings multidimensional alertness.
- Clearer perceptions facilitate decision-making.
- Better comprehension of deep mysteries opens the mind.
- Queries can be solved and anything becomes possible.
- Direct guidance is available on issues that need to be faced.
- Self-esteem, self-worth and confidence are boosted.
- Increased acceptance of the self and others brings overall harmony and peace.
- The capacity to love unconditionally is increased.

- Appreciation and respect for nature emanates the ideal atmosphere for the world to heal itself.
- An extraordinary sense of being protected and watched over provides reassurance.
- Actions are more meaningful and effective. Knowing about cause and effect gives a clearer picture of how one event connects with another.
- Progress is enhanced through self-empowering energies.
- General stability and restored faith ensure personal development.
- A consistent and reliable invisible friend is always available.
- The opportunity for healing and inner curing is magnified and accelerated.
- An essential oneness with all of life is brought about.
- Access to the wealth and abundance of Universal wisdom and Truth brings enrichment on all levels.
- Life becomes simpler, happier and requires less effort.

Although the enormity of this gift makes it impossible to fully appreciate, it should always be valued.

CHANNELLING HEALING ENERGIES

Is it possible to heal through channelling?

Modern medicine and surgery are channelled techniques that rely predominantly on physical substances and implements. However, not so long ago, healing practices simply involved prayer and the laying on of hands. Today, the increase of 'incurable' diseases simply means that there may be nothing in the physical world that can generate the healing required. The most powerful **cure** and ultimate remedy can be found through soul searching, and lies **within** the mind, body and soul. Once a connection is made with the Divine spirit, supreme resources become immediately available for healing to take place.

Why are ancient remedies so important?

There is a trend towards ancient therapies, such as massage, reflexology and aromatherapy, for the efficient release of tension and anxiety. The caressing strokes of another's hands create beneficial physical, chemical, emotional and spiritual environments that facilitate the healing process and promote general wellbeing. When relaxed, body, mind and soul become an open channel for the uninhibited flow and distribution of essential life sustaining forces

from the Universal source. The greatest healing tools always have been, and always will be, kindness, gentleness and faith. It takes only one loving thought for the healing to begin.

What makes a healing channel effective?

Being oneself is the most effective healing channel since the Divine Spirit can channel through the Creative Force for natural spontaneous healing, regeneration and rejuvenation to occur. Unseen Universal energies penetrate atomic matter and adjust the cell's memory to fine-tune the whole to resonate with the Universal energies. Healing comes from within and so healers and channellers can only restore themselves through utilisation of Universal energies. By attuning themselves to the Infinite source they can become conduits for others, allowing the recipient to adjust accordingly and become more receptive.

How does the body heal itself?

All perceptions and feelings immediately influence the consciousness within each atom of every specialised cell. All these infiltrate the body, since rotary forces within the heart of the atom alter their spin of energy and become instantly telepathic with all atoms. Any change in consciousness affects the vibrations and immediately adjusts the characteristics and condition of all atoms and cells, as well as the overall state of the body. Focusing on an ideal accelerates the process until every atom resonates in harmony with the creative life force itself. Although abundant Universal energy is always available, the interference of wilful thoughts can alter or limit it at any time. Even unhindered energy may not be fully applied and appreciated, due to of self-doubt or extreme fear of the consequences.

has any research been carried out on natural healing?

Nuclear physicist Elizabeth Rauscher tested the ability of gifted healer Olga Worsel in enhancing or retarding the growth of bacteria in special laboratory containers. It was discovered that development could be significantly affected either way at will. The bacteria were then placed in biochemical environments that either delayed or hastened their progress, but, through touch, Olga appeared to counteract the effect regardless of the chemical factors.

Does anything specific threaten personal wellbeing?

Feelings of inadequacy may cause killer T-cells to form that eventually attack healthy cells within the body. This increases vulnerability and opens the whole to an invasion of foreign substances which can highlight the volatile condition through inflammation and disease. A positive attitude and a worthwhile and fulfilling reality, on the other hand, boosts the morale and strengthens the immune system.

Exercise to experience the healing energies

Stage 1: Determining the energy.

- Rub your hands together, especially if cold, then with palms facing, place them slightly apart from one another.
- Close your eyes and concentrate on the feelings that are generated between the hands. These may be sensations of heat, vibrations or tiny invisible currents, all of which indicate the presence of vibrant Universal energy within the aura. Move the hands, as though playing an accordion, towards and away from one another in various directions and enjoy a variety of reactions.

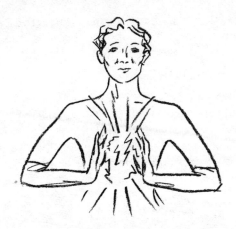

Feeling the energies between the palms

Stage 2: Sensing another soul.

● Face another person and with palms fractionally apart and eyes closed, enjoy tuning into each other's energies.

Facing another to detect each other's energies

- Determine whether the vibrations are lively, active, harmonious, tense, agitated or sluggish and then, afterwards, question one another and compare perceptions.

Stage 3: Assessing the body energies.

- Invite another person to lie flat in a relaxed position with arms and legs spread and eyes shut. With palms facing down, allow your hands to hover without touching, over the centre of their upper abdomen, where the solar plexus is situated. Close your eyes to tune into their energies and begin ascertaining their emotions.

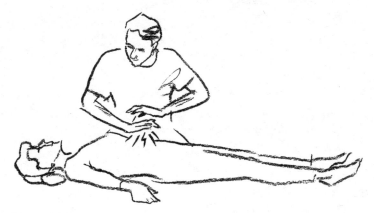

Recharging the solar plexus

- After a while, move your hands, so that one is over the other, above the centre of the forehead and stay for as long as necessary.
- Separate the hands so that each is above the eyes. Remain in this position for a while. Then with one hand over the other hover above the throat for a few seconds. Move to the space above the breastbone for as long as required. Linger over the solar plexus again. Separate the hands so that the palms are either side of the lower abdomen above the adrenal glands and then finally bring the hands together over the crutch.
- Encourage your partner, whilst still in the same position, to take in, hold and release three deep breaths before opening their

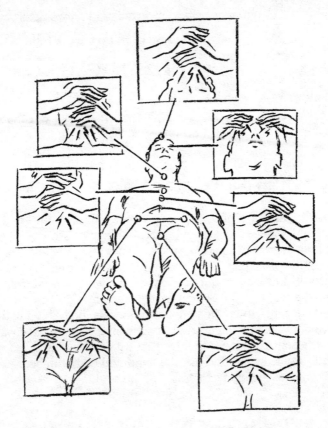

Position of all the energy centres

eyes. Once they have adjusted to the surroundings, invite them to sit up. Enquire about the sensation felt and compare your observations with their feedback.

Note: Allow the fluctuations in energy levels to determine the length of time given to each centre with extra attention being allocated to areas that feel 'starved' or 'depleted'.

Stage 4: Detect the energies of animals, plants and inanimate objects in the same way to gain an affinity with animals, nature and the environment.

CLEARING THE CHANNELS TO CHANNEL

WHICH CHANNELS NEED TO BE CLEARED?

The personality functions physically, emotionally, mentally and spiritually, with each level containing habitual patterns of response that are intimately connected to various stages of experience. The body encompasses the physical level and is brought to life by the spirit according to the amount of energy and effervescence being released. The mind, as the builder, shapes the physique through its ideas and concepts and ultimately determines the body's condition. Once free of wasteful thoughts and burdensome emotions, the way is clear for the conscious mind to reconnect with the fountainhead of Universal knowledge. In this way the mind and body can become an open channel for the pure expression of the soul.

WHY IS PURIFICATION IMPORTANT?

Purging the body and mind of wasteful energies opens the way to a source of information that is vaster and richer than could ever be humanly imagined and channelling helps to reclaim this wisdom for enrichment on every level. Through modification or elimination of all inhibiting thoughts and emotions, a weight is lifted from the mind and body, setting the soul free. Once wholesome and relaxed, the body is an ideal receptacle for Divine energy and Universal wisdom. It can be likened to a well-tuned television set that receives many channels and functions effectively.

Exercises to clear the physical body

The physical body can only be prepared for what the soul is ready to express in consciousness. To that end:

- periodically enjoy a fruit juice or purified water fast for a day or longer;
- always keep the home and garden clean and tidy, with everything in good working condition, repainting whenever necessary;
- repair or throw out defective items and give away any unused items.

The condition of property reflects the state of the body, mind and soul since every part represents and characterises specific aspects.

Room	Organ
Kitchen	Prepares and supplies energy and heat, and is equipped with cleansing facilities, similar to the assimilation, metabolic and purification processes of the **liver**.
Lounge	The love and joy that emanate from the **heart** of the home determine the amount of peace and harmony.
Dining room	Order and self-control have a balancing effect like the **spleen**.
Bedrooms	Space for personal emotions and belongings which represents the **lungs**.
Bathrooms	Filter and eliminate all wasteful aspects, which cleanses the whole, similar to the **kidneys**.

Sinks and drains symbolise the **lymphatic system**; the sewers, the **excretory systems**; the electricity, **nervous system** and so on. The atmosphere within the home is influenced by personal thoughts and emotions and vice versa. A cluttered environment reflects confusion

within the body and mind, which causes energy flow blockages, malfunctioning and unnecessary wear and tear, whilst obsessive tidiness prevents full utilisation of all the facilities, creating a strain. The garden, meanwhile, provides space for personal growth, development and well being, with too much growth causing unnecessary obstacles that hinder progress, whereas too much order is restricting. Life is a balance with the extremes being detrimental to wellbeing.

Is fasting important?

The amount of abuse through rotten thoughts, detrimental feelings, harmful words and damaging deeds determines the degree of tolerance and sensitivity towards life's circumstances, which, in turn, influences the choice of food, its intake, digestion and the eventual absorption of nutritional substances. The essence of fasting, therefore, is not in the abstinence of food but in setting aside the intense need to be intellectually and emotionally in control. There are a number of liberating techniques, such as reflexology, body massage, Hatha Yoga, Reiki and others that encourage elimination of toxic substances. Chanting, music and controlled breathing are all ways of enhancing awareness of the body's potential for attunement.

Exercise for physical relaxation

Throughout the day be conscious of the amount of distress accumulating within the body. From time to time:

- Take in deep breaths, fill the lungs with large quantities of air and hold for as long as possible. Slowly exhale allowing the tension and anxiety to seep from the body.
- Loosen up regularly by tightening and then relaxing specific muscles, particularly those in the neck. Hunch the shoulders, roll them and then slowly drop them. Pull the blades together, expand the chest and then relax.

- Keeping the head upright, turn it from side to side a few times. Allow it to drop forwards and nod smoothly up and down. Leave the chin against the chest, slowly raise it towards the right shoulder, bring it back to the centre and lift it towards the left shoulder. Repeat as often as necessary to feel the tension melt away.
- Without moving the head, exercise the eyes by looking upwards and downwards, from side to side, diagonally across to each corner in turn, then roll and finally blink.
- Lift the arms above the head, pull the torso upwards and stretch.
- At least once a day, lie flat on the floor and consciously relax the whole body from top to toe for a few minutes.

What effect does television have on the body?

Television either has subtle or intensely profound consequences. Crude sex and violence activate or upset the hormonal system, whilst fear, anger and frustration over-stimulate the adrenal glands. Atrocious acts of cruelty can cause anxiety, fury or disappointment, lower the immunity and reduce the sense of concern leading to possible behavioural pattern changes or insomnia. Conversely, programmes that are light-hearted, loving and humorous boost the immune system and decrease susceptibility to disease. To change channels, 'tell-a-vision' of how you wish your life to be. Write the script and act in the lead role making it beneficial for all those taking part, leaving the ending open to a wealth of exciting and fortunate possibilities. This can be continued at any stage. After all, the body is the theatre in which the soul enacts its role. Since matter follows thought, our physical reality is created and shaped accordingly.

The spiritual aspect

How much spiritual involvement is there?

Every soul is a miniature projection of the Creator's greater Universal Soul and although each is individual and unique, all are one in spirit with one other and the Creator. Channelling accesses other dimensions of experience for a greater awareness and understanding of our multidimensional state. When the soul's needs are ignored or restricted to the physical realm, the discontent causes individuals to search for alternatives. Alcohol, a spirit form, and/or consciousness expanding drugs abet ethereal experiences through loss of inhibition and release from daily constraints. This can result in unusual, apparently unruly and sometimes violent antisocial behaviour. Imposition of restraining laws creates further frustration and, in extreme situations, leads to drug abuse and possible addiction. Channelling and Universal guidance break the vicious cycle through the discovery of an effective outlet for the often highly developed senses. We are currently undergoing a period of great spiritual unfolding during which extensive Universal knowledge about the self and others can be attained.

Exercise to understand the role of the soul

- Imagine every soul to be a water droplet in the ocean with each being a miniature ocean in its entirety. As the water evaporates and rises to form a part of a cloud, it condenses and falls back to earth in the form of rain. The droplet is absorbed by the earth and drawn up through the roots into the plant.
- An animal devours the vegetation and the water, and is absorbed during the digestive process. It travels around the body assisting in the formation of energy, synthesis, growth and development until excreted into a river. From here it flows back into the ocean.

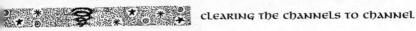

- Set your imagination free as your droplet embarks on another adventure in life such as snow on top of a mountain or as fluid refreshment for a bird and so on.

As an integral part of the Universe, all souls have intimate knowledge of the whole of creation. Through terrestrial and extra-terrestrial experiences, each soul becomes re-acquainted with itself and others to discover more about its contribution within the Universe. Being psychic is consequently an inherent and natural attribute of all souls.

What generally happens to the soul during sleep?

Life is evaluated through personal hopes and fears, but the soul has the added advantage of insight gained from a wider context in time and space. It relates to ideals learnt during previous lifetimes and applies these to its present purpose on the Earth plane. This is easier when the Conscious mind is resting during sleep, as well as through channelling.

Exercise to expand awareness of the soul

Consciousness of spirit increases self-confidence through greater self-awareness and deeper understanding of the soul's purpose on Earth.

- Visualise watching traffic from a helicopter and notice how the overall movement can be observed. The clear vision of all the various routes provides a knowledge of occurrences in the past and possibilities in the future, according to the position in the present, which provides overall comprehension of the situation. Meanwhile the participants are only aware of their individual role and immediate surroundings from their current position.

29

- Likewise the soul has a broad perspective of all dimensions, especially during sleep, when these visions are translated into dreams.

CREATING A LIFE GUIDE POSTER

WHAT IS A LIFE GUIDE POSTER?

This is a fun, meaningful and powerful way to clarify direction, especially at times of confusion and despair. It helps illustrate ideals, ambitions and innermost feelings for the soul's mission on earth to be fully realised.

EXERCISE IN PRODUCING A LIFE GUIDE POSTER

Preparation

- Buy some large colourful cardboard and gather together crayons, paints, pieces of material, sequins, glitter, tin foil or any other medium that you enjoy creating with. The poster may be square, rectangular or circular and can be based on the Feng Shui design to facilitate the advantageous flow of life-force energies.
- If you wish, use symbols, such as hearts and roses for love, doves for peace, a bird flying out of the open hand for freedom of spirit, stars for fame and so on.
- Elements reveal the various aspects of the soul.

  For example:

  Ether, in the form of a thought bubble, shows the content of the mind.
  Air represents the environment, feelings of self-esteem and self-worth as well as emotions and space.
  Fire generates enthusiasm, energy and action.

Water facilitates communication and relationships.
Earth provides a solid foundation for personal growth and development.

- Colours symbolise a variety of moods and emotions.

For example:

Gold and **silver** represent Universal abundance and enrichment on all levels.
White is for purity of spirit and reflects the angelic realm.
Purple, **indigo** and **violet** raise the level of consciousness for increased awareness.
Blue is soothing and enhances communication.
Green provides space within the environment for unlimited joy.
Pink is the colour of unconditional love.
Yellow energises and puts ideas into action.
Orange is for pleasure and delight.
Red enriches and expands.

- If you have your own ideas of how to proceed, ignore the rest of the instructions. The following guidelines are for those who are uncertain as to how to continue. Whilst reading the suggestions, jot down anything else that comes to mind and draw rough sketches to illustrate your thoughts.
- The poster can be divided roughly into nine portions as follows. It may help to write the suggestions as illustrated on the next page.
- The lower central portion represents your career pathway and mission in life. Water facilitates the flow and deep reds or maroons provide solidarity. Other possibilities include a rising phoenix or a butterfly spreading its wings to symbolise the emergence of the true self.
- The bottom left-hand corner can be created into a sanctuary of peace and a haven of calm for the attainment of Universal knowledge and profound wisdom. Open space in this area facilitates the union between your true spirit and the ultimate source of intelligence. Various shades of soft greens encourage self-acceptance whilst a mixture of gentle blues provides tranquillity and reconciliation. Earthly textures, such as minute pebbles and enriched sand, offer substantial grounding.

Wealth	Fame and illumination	Marriage
Ancestors and family	Health	Future plans
Knowledge and contemplation	Career pathway	Helpful people

The square layout

The circular plan

- In the lower right-hand corner, photographs, pictures or drawings of helpful people and inspirational souls such as guides and angels can be placed to show appreciation and acknowledgement of their assistance. White and yellow with metallic textures, like tin foil, tiny magnetic chips or metal shavings, can assist in attracting these guiding lights.
- The centre of the poster is for abundant health and vitality. A white lotus with yellow rays of vibrant light interspersed with golden sand is a possibility or a snake that symbolises the Kundalini.
- The area to the left of this can be dedicated to the source of all wisdom with memorabilia of past events, such as pictures of the first day at school, receiving certificates and awards, influential family members, teachers, ancestors and anyone who has made a deep impression. The element of wood, through the use of pieces of bark, cork or sawdust symbolises the Tree of Life with rich shades of turquoise adding depth to this profound section.
- To the right of the central portion, depict forthcoming dreams. ambitions and futuristic plans, no matter how ridiculous or improbable. Use the childlike ability to allow your imagination to run wild. Have fun. Build castles in the sky and use a mixture of bright colours plus glitter to bring it all to life. Glue on a lucky charm or special coin.
- The top right-hand corner is for joy and peace to celebrate everything coming together through complete acceptance. Two doves, two hearts or two swans and so on with shades of soft reds, pinks and whites and calm water features demonstrate the unity whilst earthly elements provide ongoing substantiality.
- The top left-hand corner attracts Universal abundance on every level through golden and silver visions of intellectual, emotional, spiritual and physical enrichment, highlighted with glitter. Rainbows, pots of gold, stars and cosmic forces symbolise unlimited resources, ongoing wealth and the presence of endless assets.
- Finally, the centre top reveals the fruition and fulfilment of all your dreams with a fiery element that generates passion, enthusiasm and energy to make anything and everything possible. A lack of symbols in this space keeps all options open.

8 THE CHANNEL OF THOUGHT

What is a thought?

Every thought or image is a projection of the mind that is an invisible force brought to life by the imagination and made visible through implementation and action. All thoughts are drawn from the Universal source of intelligence and, therefore, no thought is original since it has been recalled, adapted, refined and released many times before. Tuning into the galactic wavelength through channelling automatically links the mind with the source of supreme intelligence. Throughout history, renowned quotes have been attributed to certain individuals who are not, in fact, the origin but purely the conduits for this Universal wisdom. Their contribution, however, is important in making the sayings generally acceptable.

Where are ideas stored?

The Akashic Records, referred to as the Library of Universal Thoughts, contain a massive collection of ideas and intelligence that have been accumulated and preserved since humans first began to think. These are chronicled according to their current form to be borrowed, reconsidered, activated, spurned, changed or, hopefully, enhanced to benefit human progress and development, which is why, when searching for ideas, the eyes generally look upwards, draw together, close or have a glazed appearance. All perceptions are readily assessable for examination, re-examination, renewal or revision for the worldwide updating of evolutionary brainpower. An infinite example of this is the popular belief that 'many heads are better than one'.

how can registered thoughts be changed?

Human perceptions can be altered at any time by anyone, simply through a change of mind. For example, if the initial reaction to an intensely infuriating situation is one of anger, a solution can be sought from within, instead of outwardly apportioning blame. Having another viewpoint provides greater comprehension, which significantly alters the pattern of thought to, hopefully, one of unconditional love and greater understanding. The revised concept returns to the library and is catalogued according to its higher and more compassionate vibrations. It is now available to another thoughtful soul with one, less angry, option available.

how about inbred ideas?

Inherited belief systems are based on received information that has been accepted without question over time until, eventually, a habitual mental pattern forms that is devoid of flexibility.

> Imagine a mother filling a large fresh aubergine (egg plant) with delicious delicacies and then cutting off either end before placing it in the pan for baking. When this is questioned by her young daughter, the mother admits that she has no explanation, but is simply following her mother's method. The grandmother, equally unable to explain, says that she too has always copied her mother. The great grandmother, when asked in turn, replies with amusement that she never had a pan large enough to accommodate the whole aubergine.

One of the main reasons for inherent beliefs is extreme insecurity arising from social pressure and dogma, making it seem difficult to consider or accept other options. Just as angry thoughts can change with the penetration of enhanced vibrations at atomic level, which adjust the cell memory, so too can inherent thought patterns.

Do universal concepts ever change?

Ancient wisdom and Universal knowledge remain constant since they contain Divine Intelligence. Whosoever contacts this wisdom today will find that it is exactly the same as it was a few thousand years ago and will be a few thousand years hence since its essence never alters, although social concepts about it do. The wealth of precious knowledge available can be obtained at any time simply by making mind, body and soul openly receptive.

How are thoughts generated?

The thought process is sparked by anything of interest, be it said in conversation, read in a book, detected in the environment, heard through music, observed in nature and so on. These external stimuli are the catalysts that trigger a myriad of senses through touch, sight, smell, sound and taste. Awareness and conceptual familiarity of thoughts are generated through curiosity and stored in the Subconscious mind to be brought to the Conscious mind as required. When registered at this level the concept appears 'mind blowing' with the outcome perceived to be a 'brainwave', 'brilliant idea' or 'spark of inspiration'. Those adept at doing this are considered to be exceptionally bright and brainy. Once extracted, the idea may be kept indefinitely by the 'borrower' and accepted, utilised, changed, rejected or expanded. It then requires an outlet or channel to make an impression and generate further ideas. Once it had been activated, everything within its vicinity is affected.

How do thoughts affect us?

Thoughts determine and shape life events and circumstances. For example, politicians' thoughts, once considered and implemented as law, impose social restraints that change the course of social history.

All thoughts, therefore, need to be carefully reviewed since detrimental thoughts are destructive forces that when contained, can become malignant. On the other hand concepts of unconditional love and innate understanding sustain, nurture and encourage personal wellbeing, boost immunity, increase self-esteem and confidence and make ongoing progress possible.

How do perceptions affect the condition of the body?

'We are what we think'. Physical, chemical and intellectual conditions are greatly influenced by the patterns of thought, which adjust the passage of spiritual energy from the Universe as it enters the body. These altered energy forms penetrate the cells and become encoded at atomic level with the memory of this pattern, known as the 'etheric' or 'imaginative force', until there is a change of mind. In this way, mind, body and spirit can either be a channel of joy and immense creativity, or one of misery and self-destruction.

What is the overall effect?

Thoughts are powerful tools that make an immediate impression on others. As they develop within the mind, their vibrations send out a series of signals that extend to create an impact on everything and everyone within that thought, with the consequences depending on its forcefulness and sincerity. Once activated, its energies evaporate into outer space, powerfully influencing atmospheric and weather patterns. Climatic conditions therefore reflect the overall tone and mood of a country and vice versa. Instead of allowing environmental conditions to affect thoughts, it is possible to use thoughts to affect the conditions. The planet will then become the enriched place it is meant to be.

What is the purpose of Universal concepts?

Since the dawn of time messages from the Divine source have been repeated, either consciously or at random to help take a weight off the mind, body and soul. The progressive easing of the load allows hope, peace and unconditional love to be spread, whilst lightness of being makes way for ultimate enlightenment and self-empowerment, both of which soothe the transition into the next dimension.

Why is Divine inspiration necessary?

Certain innovative concepts are made available through several sources to ensure general awareness. Several people have the rightful claim to be channelling through the same historical wisdom although the actual contents and interpretation can vary considerably depending on the channeller's experience and comprehension of the knowledge. When enthusiastically shared in an unassuming manner, with little or no credit taken, the process is greatly accelerated with an even greater amount of information being entrusted.

What about geniuses?

Those perceived as geniuses know how to access the store of Universal wisdom but are not always too sure how to adapt the information to make it generally acceptable. Channelling brings the genius out in everyone and provides guidance in the adaptation of extraordinary ideas into a more meaningful form.

Why is channelling necessary?

The only choices that appear to be available are those prepared and packaged by others. The reasoning mind is limited to analysis through the senses and tends to believe that all knowledge comes from the

outer physical world, with science being the ultimate viewpoint. Channelling expands these thoughts and takes them into another dimension to ensure human development and advancement.

What is the most effective way to be a thoughtful channeller?

Many public speakers use their personal and sometimes limited viewpoints to captivate the audience's attention, whereas an outstanding presenter excites the participants' imaginations with Universal wisdom that has no bias, prejudice or presumption, just knowledge without restraint. Channelling triggers the sixth sense or intuition for this inspiration to be effortlessly gained.

The Conditioned Mind

How does conditioning affect the mind?

The mind's incredible capacity to access wisdom beyond the confines of human consciousness is hampered by ingrained beliefs and social conditioning. This results in rigidity, criticism, judgement, insecurity and dogmatism. In an attempt to obtain social approval, many people conform to majority consensus in the belief that it is safer to follow tried and tested pathways. New discoveries and individual progress, however, are only possible when the mind ventures into the vast unknown and this is achieved simply by challenging conditioned belief systems and turning within for guidance.

Are certain people more vulnerable?

The personality is a social creature that conceals one's true nature since it is the mask worn to look good and appease others. Self-doubting

thoughts and excessive worry prevent it from relaxing, resulting in thoughts of doom and gloom. With so many being in the dark, not being able to see what is going on, or having no reason to live, depression is becoming increasingly common. When feeling despondent, try noting everything that is unclear and 'post it' to the Universe for light to be thrown on the situation. The response is rarely as expected but, when it comes, it will be enlightening. Meanwhile, boost the morale by looking back to see how much of that which was once believed to be impossible has since materialised.

Exercise to expel worn-out and outdated concepts

Rigorous exercise is an excellent antidote to depressed thought patterns since high levels of exertion cause the body to secrete chemicals called endorphins, which induce a sense of exhilaration and general wellbeing. However, active housework or gardening can also be worthwhile and beneficial forms of exercise:

- Spring-clean the home from top to bottom and sort through files, dispensing with outdated papers to create space to think clearly.
- Clear the garden of weeds, undergrowth and dead vegetation, add topsoil, compost, fertiliser and water regularly. Ensure that all water features are always clean.
- In the absence of a garden, contribute to the good of the neighbourhood by offering, for example, to erase graffiti on public walls, care for the lawns, or assist weekly in the grounds of a retirement village or home for the disadvantaged.

Various levels of consciousness

how many levels of consciousness are there?

The mind is made up of many minds, with the expressions 'being in two minds' and 'making up your mind' illustrating the frequent need to choose between the intellect and the intuition. The Conscious and Unconscious minds are personal but, through the Subconscious and Higher Conscious minds, can become transpersonal and freely integrate with the Universal mind, where all minds are linked. Just as lungs partake of the same air, so it is that all minds share the same space with 'like-minded thinkers' drawing from a similar source.

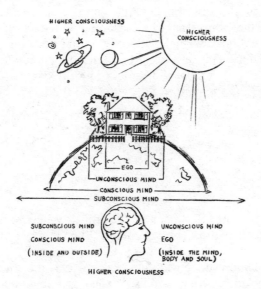

The various levels of the mind

Exercise to understand the various levels of consciousness

Visualise the following.

- The Higher Self or Greater Consciousness is the owner of a home and garden with unlimited access to the world and Universe. Its cognisance of the whole depends on its travels and development through its many lifetimes.

- The Conscious mind resides on the property and has the choice to remain confined within the boundaries or roam freely around the world. It can only view the Universe, however, through the Higher Self since its role is confined to our physical world. Its role is to select furnishings and decorations, synonymous of belief systems, collected and accumulated over the years. Extensive travel broadens its outlook and extends its options for additions or changes whilst excessive fear causes inanimate objects and worn-out belief systems to be desperately clung to. Meanwhile, items that are threatening or cannot be dealt with are tucked out of sight in the dark confines of the Subconscious mind. Unless regularly sorted out, these accumulate, take up valuable space, causing disorders and ultimately dis-ease.

- The Unconscious mind is the caretaker that keeps everything in excellent working order, twenty-four hours a day. It continually tidies and cleans up, ridding the place of rubbish and unnecessary objects. When the Conscious and Subconscious minds co-operate, everything flows smoothly but more often than not old, worn-out, useless articles are hung on to, creating extra work and wearing out the now exhausted Unconscious mind.

- The Ego, limited to staying on the property, influences the movements of the Conscious mind. When it is fearful and insecure, it entraps and restricts the consciousness, prevents it from communicating with the outside world and makes interaction with the Universe impossible. Personal growth and development are then limited, which further compounds the situation.

how does channeLLInG assIsτ τhe τhoughτ pRocess?

Channelling helps the mind to change its way of thinking by reassuring the insecure Ego, easing the Subconscious mind, freeing the conscious mind and raising the level of consciousness for greater functioning and expansive exploration. A balance between the intellect and intuition is essential otherwise the balance is tipped, causing nature to step in. For example, highly intellectual parents may have very intuitive and psychic offspring who, in extreme situations, could develop hyperactivity or autism. Meanwhile children born to 'way out' souls are often exceptionally intelligent. In both situations the two extremes can learn from one another for appropriate cognisant adjustments and equality of thought. Solutions and guidance of exactly how to do this can be obtained through channelling, from the Higher Consciousness.

BeInG a ConscIous channeL

Whaτ Is τhe RoLe oF τhe ConscIous mInd?

The whole mind is far greater and more extensive than can ever be imagined since the Conscious mind is the lowest band of the spectrum. It is used by the soul as a highly focused channel to concentrate on physical details. Its knowledge is received predominantly from the outside world, so it usually lacks far-sighted vision and for this reason is known at the 'Little Mind' at the base of the funnel.

The more rigid its perspective, the tighter, its boundaries. It actively controls the intellect and uses stored knowledge to determine the basis of all propositions presented to it. For example, if it is suggested that there is a vase of flowers on the table, when there is not, the Conscious mind immediately compares this statement with

The Conscious mind

previous impressions made by the ever-astute senses and immediately disagrees. If, asked to imagine an object, such as the vase of flowers, an exception is made and the Conscious mind steps aside to allow the Subconscious mind to conjure up the image, after which it readily accepts and complies with the appropriate image. For the Conscious mind to continue to accept this hypothetical image, a form of channelling occurs, to prevent anything else from interfering with the imagination.

bow do conditioned belief systems influence this part of the mind?

The Conscious mind operates according to the sensory-based ego with its beliefs being programmed from outside sources, as it adopts those convictions that it believes will determine the best course of action for personal survival. Channelling encourages the Conscious mind to deal with the more threatening and challenging concepts by providing options that exist beyond the obvious. In this way, disruptive thoughts are dealt with and a natural state of enhanced health is maintained.

In the dark confines of the mind

The Subconscious mind, between the Higher Conscious and Conscious minds, extends into the vast cosmic spheres, far beyond the conscious dimensions of life. It intuitively interprets all Universal impressions that are conveyed by the Super Conscious mind, and transforms extraordinary ideas in more meaningful terms. Unfortunately, this activity has become partly dysfunctional since it more commonly ends up storing disturbed thoughts that are avoided by the Conscious mind. These niggle and simmer beneath the surface and can erupt to display symptoms of discomfort which could develop into disease unless attended to. Channelling provides the tools to attain Universal wisdom and deal with all traumatic and threatening thoughts. Once past issues are seen in a different light, they are easier to resolve, leaving no unfinished business to disturb or disrupt the mind. Ultimate understanding and forgiveness, of the self and others, liberates body, mind and soul, so that at the time of death, when the Conscious mind dies with the body, the Subconscious mind can transcend in pease to the spiritual realm for safekeeping. It accompanies the soul and remains active in other dimensions of existence until manifesting in another life form, which means that the soul and Subconscious mind are always together.

Becoming acquainted with the Higher Self

What is the Higher Self?

The Higher Self is the link between the individual and Universe. It has many guises that extend way beyond the current personality, with the Conscious realm being the dimension that makes its presence known in the terrestrial world. It mediates between the

physical body and the Creator for the conscious integration of the material and spiritual aspects of life which will, ultimately, manifest in the form of one enlightened being. Through channelling, an exceptional understanding can be obtained since its wisdom and knowledge transcend the Conscious ego. Whereas most people dislike obstacles, condemn failures and deplore weakness, the Higher Self, as the wiser part of the self, views these as excellent opportunities for personal growth and greater enlightenment.

EXERCISE TO MEET YOUR HIGHER SELF

Thinking of the ideal automatically connects the Conscious channel to that of the Higher Self with access best achieved through channelling or meditation. If you wish, imagine this phenomenal essence as a Guardian Angel or someone who is very wise.

- Sit comfortably with your eyes closed and take in three deep breaths, holding each as long as possible before breathing out. Feel the physical tension seep out of the body and evaporate. Ask for Universal guidance to assist the process.
- In your mind's eye, see your Higher Self suspended in space as you wish it to be, either in spirit or as a magnificent being by visualising an angel or a glorified version of someone you greatly admire.

An angelic version of the Higher Self

- Now look at your inner being. Relax and just be. Feel your body becoming gradually more and more weightless until your spirit is able to float upwards on a soft pink cloud to become one with the all embracing Higher Self. For greater security an ethereal umbilical cord connecting your body to your Higher Self can be visualised. Enjoy the pure bliss, warmth, compassion and utter joy of timeless, ethereal non-existence and cherish the companionship felt with your Higher Self. Laugh and take comfort at being united.
- To return to your physical body watch the ethereal umbilical cord shorten or imagine a swirling spiral forming a cloud-like channel that draws your united spirit back into the body.

A swirling, cloud-like spiral

- When ready to return to the physical realm, take in three deep breaths, each time becoming more aware of the surrounding environment. Listen for familiar noises and adjust to various sensations inside and outside the body. Remain connected with your Higher Self and enjoy feeling its energy vibrating throughout you.
- Thank the Universe for its guidance and slowly open your eyes as you experience a wholesome feeling and great inner peace. Connection with the Higher Self forms a natural channel, through which a wealth of Universal knowledge is available on request.

Exercise to obtain answers from the Higher Self

The Universe helps those who help themselves, so ask specific questions and look for the answers inside the soul. If this does not come easily, then use the following exercise:

- Seat yourself comfortably and request Universal guidance. Write down questions to bring them to the front of your mind and then close your eyes and relax the physical body through the breath. Remain still and just be. Enjoy an all-embracing calmness as the mind clears and experience an inner peace as you drift into a meditative state.
- Visualise your Higher Self or a Divine image in this translucent space and allow this tranquillity to extend beyond and above you so that it becomes at one with the source of Greater Intelligence. Assume that you are in that position with an overall view of the earth and the limitless Universe.
- Now pose questions, one at a time, and be still. From this incredible vantage point consider all options and, by looking at the situation from every point of view formulate a solution. Draw on inner resources for clarification and make a mental note of everything that comes to mind.
- Take three deep breaths to return to physical reality and express gratitude for Universal assistance.

Many beautiful inspirational and angel cards are available from New Age, book and health shops. These can also provide reassurance and guidance by creating awareness of the Higher Self's ideals of complete understanding of the true self and concepts of excellence.

The Purpose of an ideal

What is an ideal?

Ideals are models of Divine perfection that are the invisible templates, or patterns, which govern the visible aspects of life. As they filter

down into more tangible forms, many of their superb qualities are lost, until eventually they only approximate the original ideal since ultimate perfection only exists in an idealised spirit form in the ethereal realm. Ideals are the currently unattainable pattern of Super Conscious perfection and the parents of all ideals. They differ from ideas in that, once an idea has been enthusiastically implemented and served its purpose, it no longer occupies the mind and loses much of its power to motivate. An ideal, on the other hand, is eternal and continually provides inspiration. Focusing on an ideal whilst channelling makes it a more purposeful, constructive and worthwhile act.

Exercise to explore your ideals

Investigate the ideal uppermost in your mind and develop a feeling for it by copying the following questions with your right hand, if right handed, or with your left, if left handed: 'What is my ideal?' 'What is the essence of my spirit?' 'What is my highest value?' 'How would I ideally like to live?' 'How can I attain ideal attributes?' Allow the opposite hand to respond. Wealth and happiness are often perceived to be the highest ideals, but both are attainable and, therefore, are ideas and not ideals. Perfect love, complete harmony and Universal peace are closer to being ideals and, when adopted, an unbelievable state of unlimited bliss is inevitable.

How is channelling influenced by an ideal?

The higher the ideal, the more profound the information that is channelled through because the wisdom attained transcends the channeller's own learning experience, ability and knowledge. It has a psychic component that resonates more powerfully. The ultimate ideal is inspired by Universal Consciousness, which is not a religion but an aspect of life. It was the total awareness, willingness, acceptance and commitment that filled every cell of their bodies,

49

that made Jesus, Buddha, Mohammed and other enlightened beings so special. In so doing, they demonstrated that all human beings can do the same and Jesus said, 'These things that I do, so shall ye, and more'. The time is right to put that prophecy into practice.

Expanding the mind

What are the advantages of having an open mind?

Channelling is a voyage of discovery that encourages ingrained beliefs to be seen in a new light. Freed from the constraints of inhibited, obsessive thoughts, self-doubt and paranoid delusions dissipate and the frustrating need to conform to outdated belief systems diminishes. Tuning into cosmic wavelengths is only a thought away and becomes progressively easier until eventually it is a way of life.

Exercise to evolve the mind

You may wish to use visualisation in the following five stages.

1 Imagine yourself at the edge of a vast lake. What can you see? An indeterminable amount of water, plants, flowers, trees and much more in a landscape that extends as far as the horizon. Above is a clear blue sky with sporadic white clouds. Birds fly overhead or settle momentarily on the reeds and branches, whilst butterflies flit here and there and an intrepid rabbit peeks from behind a rock and then hops back into its burrow out of view. Allow your vivid imagination to continue. Then imagine the scene from another side of the lake. Ponder upon the delicate details of nature, such as the shape and colours of each leaf yet feel the resilience and strength of it all. Appreciate the valuable role of everything seen and marvel at the exquisite textures of the

unfolding scene, noting that, no matter how diverse, everything is so beautifully interlinked.

2 In your mind's eye go under water to discover the intensity of this dark and mysterious fluid world that teems with distinctive life forms, all of which contribute in their own way to the pattern of life.

3 Next envisage yourself looking down at the lake from the summit of a nearby mountain. Notice the vastness of the expanse of water. This can now be observed in its entirety and yet it appears to be so small. Everything within the lake can only be imagined. So much more of the landscape is visible from this elevated position with objects once out of sight, now becoming apparent.

4 Visualise the same scene from a cloud. The lake, previously a massive expanse of water, can still be perceived but seems so insignificant when compared with its surroundings. Its position, however, in the neighbouring countryside is easier to understand.

5 Now take your mind into outer space. The lake becomes even less discernible until it is eventually a mere speck that is increasingly indistinguishable from the surrounding landmass. Stars and planets that were barely visible reveal the earth to be only one of billions of cosmic forms.

Many ideas and thoughts may have come to mind whilst doing this exercise but consider also some of the following:

● Although no more than an infinitesimal speck in the Universe, each individual has a vital and significant role to play. Every thought, feeling and action has an incredible impact upon the finer details of life that ultimately affect the whole. What better way to illustrate this than to recall the importance of the billions upon billions of microscopic cells which constitute our own bodies.

● The Universe has in-depth comprehension of the extreme importance of each and every living cell. This magnificent vastness allows it to fathom the infinite significance of each tiny dust particle as well as the immense complexity of the planets in outer space. The depth of this knowledge is still beyond the grasp of human perception and continues to remain an intriguing mystery.

● With such diversity within human nature, experience, traditions and language, it is inevitable that acknowledgement of the

Divine source will embrace a multitude of beliefs. All are one and the same. This extraordinary Universal source defies a single description since it is anything and everything. Guidance and encouragement are constantly available but free will determines whether it is fully appreciated or employed.

- With changes occurring as the soul moves on, the angle or position at any given moment ascertains the many points of view as progress is made. If something is not visible or distinguishable, it does not mean that it does not exist. Likewise the Universe does not need to be seen to be believed.

Through channelling, the guidance obtained from a magnificent source allows absolute comprehension of all aspects of life, no matter how minuscule or immense, which opens the mind to numerous concepts with inexhaustible options.

EXERCISE TO EXTEND CONCEPTS BEYOND CONDITIONED BELIEF SYSTEMS

When receiving information, question it and test it for its authenticity. Consider it from every point of view. For example:

Question: If ultra-violet light from the sun is a real cause of skin cancer, why does this malignant disease develop in only some of those who have been exposed to the solar rays as well as in others who have avoided them or taken extensive precautions?

Answer: Cancer may arise from suppressed anger, frustration and discontent that, over a period of time, becomes contained and begins to grow. The amount of sensitivity within the skin may depend on environmental conditions. It could be argued that skin cancer arises from covering up the true self in perceivably unfavourable environmental situations. Physical symptoms could be merely the messengers that draw attention to the need to acknowledge and deal with the root causes.

Question: Is the hole in the ozone layer, perceived to be so detrimental, in fact throwing light on planetary issues and drawing attention to current situations that need to be faced for ultimate enlightenment?

Question: Would there be life without the sun?

Question: How can you continue to expand these questions?

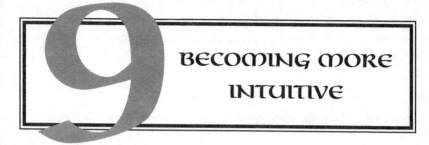

BECOMING MORE INTUITIVE

WHAT IS INTUITION?

Intuition remains a mystery and a challenge. This knowing sensation appears to have no reason since it is an uncanny feeling, 'gut reaction' or 'knowing in the bones' that serves as a warning to do or not do something. This intense desire and compelling need is often referred to as 'coincidence' since it is not a creation of the conscious mind but an invisible channel of knowledge that draws upon the unfathomable source of infinite wisdom providing guidance through psychic awareness.

HOW DOES INTUITION WORK?

The intuitive mind functions through attunement, achieved through the empathetic adjustment of two energies which merge and essentially become part of one another. With this harmonious resonance and communion, there is an immediate link with the Universal source.

WHO IS INTUITIVE AND WHY IS IT IMPORTANT?

Anyone with a great imagination is intuitive since creative images are important channels of revelation. Intuition instinctively protects

the soul and provides reliable guidance in personal and business affairs.

How believable is the process?

Questions contain vibrations that have the seeds of the answers. As queries are posed, answers immediately spring to mind but are frequently set aside as being ridiculous, impossible or unbelievable. These more natural, empathetic responses need to be trusted for insight to be attained.

How are intuitive solutions obtained?

The intuitive channel spontaneously responds when attuned to the core being, although the type of reply varies considerably. Socrates, the ancient Greek philosopher, frequently referred to the Divine voice that he heard. Although hearing voices is generally perceived to be a sign of madness, everyone has an inner voice that participates in 'mind-talk'.

How can intuition be trusted?

The first thing that comes to mind is so quickly judged, evaluated and modified that it rapidly dissipates. You can overcome this by keeping the first response in mind and saving evaluation for later. This involves having confidence in natural, spontaneous impulses, at a level of faith and self-acceptance that is generally resisted. Belief in the process allows issues to be spontaneously understood as a relationship forms with the part of the self that is completely trustworthy.

What is the difference between the conscious and intuitive minds?

Intuitive responses are unpredictable whilst conscious responses, being habitual, are more predictable. When interjected mind-talk is surprisingly sympathetic, it is more likely to be the intuition, which does not criticise or condemn but grasps the underlying motive and offers assistance.

What is the 'sixth sense'?

Intuition is also known as the 'sixth sense', which refers to its mystical and psychic characteristics. When appearing to be 'unreasonable' or 'not making sense', individuals are asked to 'come to their senses', the effect of which often causes a feeling of shame or embarrassment. If ridicule is experienced when using intuition or too much intellect is involved, the conscious mind becomes inhibited and severs its link with the Higher Conscience, closing off this essential part of the mind. It is then impossible to access the Universe or telepathically connect with other minds.

How can intuition be activated?

Learning to function intuitively is instinctive and cannot be taught but it can be advantageously cultivated as an everyday channel of guidance. This is best achieved through relaxation and by directing the attention within, although some of the most intuitive experiences are unexpected and spontaneous. The unconditional acceptance of the self and others is the most effective tool for ultimate synchronisation.

Exercise to improve intuition

Nature assists in developing an innate awareness of the Universe and a profound relationship with the meaning of life.

- Spend more time outside to tune into the natural cycles of life so that your resonance can adapt to nature's vibrations.
- Birds are an expressive form of the soul's spirit and convey telepathic and intuitive messages – 'A little bird told me so'. In the Bible, the Holy Spirit appears as a dove.
- Plants can be more intuitively understood through appreciation of their exquisite, yet simplistic, parts.

Is it possible to become more psychic?

Trusting intuition can develop innate psychic powers. Extra sensory perception (ESP) is one of the highest forms of psychic ability since it brings with it subliminal premonition.

Channelling through ideas with imagination

Where do ideas come from?

Experience provides a platform for ideas but is not their source since they exist in another dimension beyond time and space. Tuning into an idea shapes personal experiences and encourages each individual to create their own reality. Ideas are on loan to everyone but belong to no one since they are part of the Universal mind.

What is imagination?

The imagination is a channel of psychic sensitivity and visionary perception, with the imagery being the language of the Subconscious mind. It is the process by which life is experienced in patterns rather than in a linear, logical form, thereby determining the state of the body

and steering most activities. These etheric or imaginative forces within the mind are designed to motivate and exert their influence in the precipitation of new ideas so that they can be translated into action.

EXERCISE USING THE IMAGINATION

Ask your mouth to salivate and see the response. Now imagine yourself on a very hot day and notice how parched your mouth becomes until you can take no more, and have to have a long drink of icy cold water. Experience the relief of the cool, refreshing liquid as it moistens the lips, soothes the tongue and caresses the back of the throat. Relish the sensation of utter joy.

WHY IS IMAGINATION SO IMPORTANT?

A thought makes us think but an image touches and affects our whole being. Consider how children employ imagination when playing games or acting out their fantasies. The reality comes from being so totally absorbed in all that is being done, in the same way that the ethereal elements of life can be seen through psychic, intuitive vision.

EXERCISE TO DEVELOP THE IMAGINATION

The imagination expands when it is assumed that something is actually being done instead of visualising its enactment. Recall how easy it was to 'make believe' during childhood, without being concerned about the vividness of the imagination. It is through this pretence that the reality can take shape. Whilst doing the following exercise, focus less on the product and more on the process.

● Imagine being your friend, colleague, spouse, parent, child and/or pet by stepping into their position and seeing yourself from their viewpoint.
● Do you like what you see? If not, why not? What advice would you give yourself?

- Treat yourself as you would like others to and unconditionally accept and encourage yourself.
- If you like what you see, appreciate yourself and consider ways of becoming even more of who and what you are.
- Thank the source of Divine energy for your blessings.

Let go of all inhibitions and be inspired, to increase receptivity for psychic awareness.

EXERCISE TO CREATE A MORE VIVID IMAGINATION

Lie next to a tree and daydream, allowing your imagination to spin images and stories based on past experiences and hopes and fears for the future. Believe it to be your own private world and allow pleasing illusions to reflect a psychic influence. Thoughts of another person can exert a subliminal influence upon daydreaming patterns of others and vice versa, because all Subconscious minds are connected and have unlimited access to one another.

UNDERSTANDING MENTAL DISEASE

What causes mental disease?

Individuals become mentally ill when they are unable to bring their innermost thoughts to the fore causing them to feel lost and off track. Extreme frustration at not being understood results in these disillusioned souls mentally escaping and retreating into a world of their own. Mental illness emerges when the individual is overwhelmed by unconscious urges of extreme emotions, such as aggression or sexual impulses and when the ego is no longer able to mediate between these inner forces and the world. The lack of stability leads to hallucinations, exceptional mood swings and delusions.

How does mental illness start?

During early childhood, mentally disturbed and multiple personalities may spontaneously develop channelling abilities to escape abusive, neglected and intolerable circumstances. Their only refuge is in a secret hiding place within the imagination where the mind can be kept safe from harm. Everyone does this, to a certain extent, to escape the harsh realities of life. When the dominant characteristics of the main personality are ignored, the mind may become resentful, whilst other aspects that are more in tune with psychic abilities may break through to show 'signs of madness'. This 'insane behaviour' is considered to be a threat to society, but is generally due to lack of understanding. In the past, victims were locked away in lunatic asylums. Today, medication is prescribed to calm down victims and make them conform to socially acceptable patterns of behaviour.

Is there a connection between mental illness and channelling?

Those classified as mentally ill may exhibit unusually high psychic abilities, since habitual survival mechanisms are diminished and access is gained to information and ways of knowing that are normally screened out. In this way people with split personalities and mental disorders may stumble into intuitive states, including communication with spirit guides. Channelling may also loosen the ego structure and encourage the mind to wander into altered states of consciousness, but from a safe base. Greater understanding of the socially confined and mentally ill aspects of the multidimensional mind may be gained, through channelling, thereby increasing the likelihood of discovering a workable solution.

What does 'being possessed' mean?

Intense affinity with and attachment to a thought may make individuals so possessed with passionate desires that they become a

driving force of extreme determination, making implementation of the idea imperative. Everyone is possessed to some extent: you may have heard someone say that they are not sure what 'possessed' them to do or say something. It may arise from an overwhelming and impulsive need to act or respond uncharacteristically and illogically for no known reason at the time. With Divine guidance, a balance may be achieved.

how can channelling assist?

Through channelling, thoughts that occupy the Conscious mind may become possessed with the creative and intuitive aspects of the Subconscious mind. It is difficult to think clearly when the racing mind is filled with extreme concern, anxiety and sometimes hopelessness, but once put into perspective, solutions may come instantly to the fore. When souls are possessed with the spirit of Universal love, there is only space for peace.

Are there other means of attaining inner tranquillity?

Extreme states of calm may also be reached through natural relaxation techniques such as reflexology, meditation and yoga, during which everything may become clearer. With absolute calm, there is absolute perspective. When the water is clear and still, the bottom of the pond can be seen. Communion with the Higher Self and the Divine source is as simple as this because the absolute truth is within everyone.

Channelling through innovative concepts

Where do inspirational and innovative thoughts come from?

Thoughts, enriched by awe-inspiring wisdom, are fine-tuned vibrations that are drawn from the reference section of the Universal Library. These raise the level of consciousness and provide the clarity of vision required to perceive future concepts and their ultimate development. The Ten Commandments, the Book of Revelations and many other such expedient concepts are examples of this wisdom, as are the remarkable inventions and advanced technology that have ensured ongoing development. Everything was once a thought and was pictured in the mind long before becoming a reality with all ideas coming from a greater source.

Channelling and hypnosis

What happens during hypnosis?

Hypnosis facilitates direct communication with the Subconscious mind, through a heightened state of suggestibility that causes it to accept any statement made to it as being true. As the sensory system becomes less agitated and the consciousness is less defensive, the now uninhibited Subconscious can use its vivid imagination to make the suggestions real within the mind.

Is it possible to hypnotise oneself?

Hypnosis and meditation are very similar, except that whilst in the hypnotic state responses can be made to self-induced suggestions. Self-hypnosis is best learnt through expert guidance and assistance.

Practising Meditation

What is Meditation?

Meditation, referred to as the fourth level of consciousness, is an ancient art that effectively prepares the body, mind and soul for enhanced guidance from the Divine source. It is a spiritual tool with such amazing benefits that it is often medically prescribed to treat stress-related issues. Inner peace allows the consciousness to attain greater wisdom since the cells automatically adjust and absorb the pattern of these enlightened energies. As spiritual awareness increases, individuals become channels of inspiration through whom the breath of life, the Spirit, can flow freely. Meditation is excellent for personal wellbeing and an ideal way of opening up to the Creator, spirit guides, angels and other ethereal entities.

Why Meditate?

There is a great wide world and an even greater outer space awaiting exploration, much of which is way beyond general comprehension. Meditation takes the mind beyond the obvious into the unknown by calming it down and aligning it with the source of Universal wisdom. As slow-moving alpha waves take over, thoughts can escape beyond the boundaries of the personality to access an elevated realm of awareness, where the soul can rediscover its true essence for a more manageable and fulfilling reality.

Is it Easy to Meditate?

Meditation is an innate skill that can be easily reclaimed. The mind simply transcends its physical mass, passes through various levels of consciousness and breaks free into the extensive ethereal realm of wisdom. This can be likened to a water bubble rising from the ocean floor until it bursts through the expanse above and dissipates to become part of the vast unknown.

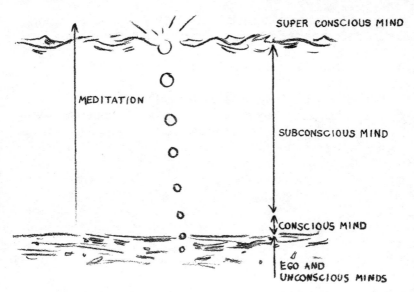

SUPER CONSCIOUS MIND

MEDITATION

SUBCONSCIOUS MIND

CONSCIOUS MIND

EGO AND
UNCONSCIOUS MINDS

The process of meditation

Which is the best technique?

Everyone has their own method of meditation that can be modified at will since only the individual can define their unique path for unfolding. Once attuned to the Spirit, it is natural to psychically evolve and become spiritually awakened. All that is required is to trust the intuition to provide guidance which is particularly effective when tuned into the highest vibration. To permit the free flow of the spirit, surround yourself with bright white light, focus on your ideal and concentrate on your breathing.

What happens to the body?

During meditation every cell of the body aligns itself with the pattern of energy that is being channelled through. This effectively reduces oxygen consumption and carbon dioxide elimination

causing the rate and volume of respiration to decrease. The body becomes very still and is infiltrated by an inner sense of peace and wellbeing.

Are there different levels of meditation?

The type of Universal wisdom accessed and channelled through depends on the current level of consciousness. This is determined by the stage of personal development since spiritual energies are magnetically drawn by the predominant thoughts that occupy the mind. As the pattern of Divine energy penetrates the body it alters terrestrial intelligence and becomes encoded into the cellular awareness of the body to shift consciousness and ensure progression.

What is a mantra?

A mantra is a sound, which is constantly repeated to help quieten the mind. Certain tones and words such as *Om* and *Rama*, chosen from the Sanskrit language, have been identified as having a soothing effect that raises the level of consciousness. Their real power lies in their vibrational frequencies, which link the cells of the body to the melody of life and attune them to the realms of light and space.

Exercise in meditation

It may help to record these instructions on to an audio tape which will also assist in controlling the required length of time allocated to meditation. Use low, soothing tones with soft, gentle music in the background.

Method 1

● Sit comfortably with your eyes closed and ask for Universal guidance.

- Choose a word or simple image that fills you with joy and concentrate on this and nothing else. If you picked 'happy' simply think of that word over and over again. If you chose a 'balloon', picture this in your mind. Keep looking at it and nothing else.
- At first other words, pictures or distractions might intrude. If they do, acknowledge them and them return your attention to the chosen subject. Just keep focused.
- Be aware of a mindfulness that feels familiar and is always in the background at the back of the mind. It is the silent 'I' that tends to be dominated by the 'ego'. This silent 'I' is the 'I am', 'I am awareness', 'I am one with the Universe and its Creator'. Meditation is the gateway to this channel of awareness.
- When ready, take in some deep breaths, and each time become more aware of the physical environment. Slowly open your eyes. Acknowledge and thank the Universe for its assistance.

Method 2

- Sit comfortably, this time with your eyes open, and request Universal guidance.
- Imagine a spot high up on the wall across from you and stare at that imaginary point. Count slowly backwards from ten to one. Start with ten and slowly say this number, in your mind, as you take in a deep breath. As you exhale, leisurely blink your eyelids. Repeat with nine, blink, then eight, blink, and so on. Each time allow your eyelids to become very heavy and extremely relaxed.
- Allow this feeling to spread in imaginary waves or ripples throughout your face, around your head, down your neck and throat, along the shoulders and throughout your entire body until completely at ease. Feel your mind, body and soul relax bit by bit, then deeper and deeper, and savour the inner peace, total tranquillity and complete harmony of total relaxation. Relish the opportunity to let go. Enjoy being at one with your Creator. Just be.
- When ready to return to the conscious part of your mind, repeat the deep breathing procedure but this time, count in reverse, from one to ten. Feel yourself readjust as terrestrial senses take

over. Gradually open your eyes and be still until your vision focuses. Thank your Guides for their assistance.

What can be learnt from these techniques?

In meditation there is always a focal point, be it a sound, word, sentence, image, breath or thought, which can be used to establish a direct link with the Universe. The initial conflict between the intention to stay centred and the mind's natural tendency to stray and amuse itself with spontaneous activity will, in time, dissipate. With frequent meditation, these two forces meet and gradually negate one another until all that remains is the presence of 'I am' awareness, which is the channel of complete attainment.

Exercise to understand the process of meditation

- Sit comfortably with your eyes closed and ask for Universal guidance.
- Imagine an area of bright light above and just behind the head, at the point where many feel the presence of the Higher Self. Visualise it to be like a hood of hallowed energy that is often depicted on saintly beings.
- Concentrate on this source of energy, draw from it and merge with it until you feel part of it, suspended in mid air. Appreciate this space and give yourself time to enjoy its energy.
- When you are ready, return to the confines of the body. Re-acquaint yourself with the physical environment through controlled breathing. Acknowledge the Divine assistance.

Each and every experience during this exercise is unique with hearing sounds, seeing colours, experiencing visions and feeling cold being some of the sensations evoked. Less common are aches, tingling, shaking, vibrations, emotional stirrings and so on as body, mind and soul become aware of their inner being.

A hallowed energy form

EXERCISE TO MEDITATE ON THE BREATH

Before meditating on the breath, it is useful to practise various forms
of breathing to determine the method that is most comfortable. If
you have never meditated before, you may prefer to approach the
technique in stages. To facilitate the procedure record the
instructions on to an audio tape, using soft soothing tones and
gentle music in the background.

Stage 1

- Sit comfortably with your eyes closed and ask for Divine wisdom
  and Universal guidance to assist you at all times.
- Consciously loosen every part of the body through visualisation
  or by gripping and releasing each muscle in turn. Start with the
  feet and legs, then the hands and arms, followed by the trunk
  from the pelvis upwards, finishing with the shoulders, neck, face
  and scalp.
- Imagine a fine but strong thread attached to the top of your
  head and feel it gently but firmly pull to gradually lift the head,
  slowly raise the chin, gently stretch the neck, lengthen the spine
  and straighten the back.

- Focus on your breathing and allow it to happen effortlessly. Inhale a long deep appreciative breath. Notice how the nostrils flare, the tiny hairs vibrate and feel the tingle of energy from the air itself. Enjoy the passage of warmth down the back of the throat and visualise it caressing and soothing the walls of the air pipe. As the air divides into the two lungs, imagine it dissolving into all the nooks and crannies as the chest proudly expands to accommodate this energising life force.
- Hold the breath, savour and enjoy it as you appreciate its essence and vitality.
- Breathe out s-l-o-w-l-y. Feel all tension seep from the body, especially from the neck and shoulders. Relax.
- Now open the mouth and this time, draw the breath into the stomach. See it gushing through the teeth, wafting over the tongue, drifting down the back of the throat, passing through the oesophagus until it enters and expands the stomach, filling it to its full capacity. Hold for as long as is comfortable and then slowly breath out to completely empty the stomach as the abdominal muscles retract.
- Sense yourself relaxing more and more as you alternate the nostril/lung and the mouth/stomach breathing. If preferred, this can be in cycles, i.e. three nostril/lung breaths, followed by three mouth/stomach breaths, or three to one.
- As each breath is exhaled, become more and more aware of your inner being. Imagine air penetrating every part of the body, from the centre and spreading outwards until reaching the top of the head as well as the tips of each finger and toe. Feel energy vibrating in every cell and then be still.
- From this point of stillness, draw deeper and deeper into yourself to discover and explore all innermost sensations. Tune into these intrinsic personal vibrations and detect areas that have been starved of attention. Concentrate on each deprived area individually either by humming into it or sending it pure white light or any other colour that comes to mind.
- As you breathe in, take in thoughts of love, joy and understanding and when you breathe out consciously let go of fearful, threatening thoughts. Feel the tension dissipating and continue

this breathing until there is complete inner peace. Breathe naturally and stay in this serene space.

- When ready, either progress to **stage 2**, or move on to **stage 4**.

Stage 2

- Focus on this solitary tranquillity and bring its core into the centre of your body. From this focal point, visualise yourself as a sun burst with the most exquisite rays of gold, silver, white, purple, blue, pink, green, yellow, orange, and red in every shade imaginable.

Burst of vibrant energy

- Feel the rays of light and colour spread throughout your whole being and beyond. Imagine fine threads of vibrant energy infiltrating every molecule of the body, which then extend beyond the physical until they dissipate into space.
- At any stage, resume the breathing technique to ground and reassure yourself.
- If you wish to continue go on to **stage 3**, otherwise proceed to **stage 4**.

Stage 3

- As mind, body and soul are filled with this vibrant source, feel every particle lifting upwards, sinking downwards, expanding outwards and filtering inwards until eventually there is no physical definition between yourself and your surroundings. Even if you only partially experience this, you are doing exceptionally well. The more relaxed and secure you feel, the easier it becomes but take time to trust the process and enjoy the sensation of lightness.
- Be aware of the top of your head opening like a huge channel to embrace the whole of the Universe.

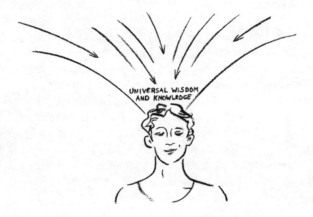

The head as an open channel

- As the Divine presence enters and Universal guidance takes over whatever is felt from this point is individual. You will be given the wisdom to know exactly what to do. Have faith.

Stage 4

- With your eyes still closed, gradually allow yourself to become increasingly aware of the immediate environment. Compare the solidity of the earth below with the space of the air above. Sense the surrounding temperature and listen for various sounds to distinguish their source. Allow enveloping odours to waft up your nose.

- Consciously take in a deep breathe, hold it for as long as possible and, as you slowly exhale, visualise the breath dissipating into the surrounding atmosphere. Use each breath to connect with your surroundings until completely aware of the immediate environs and then slowly open your eyes.
- Stay seated as your mind, body and soul as you adjust to the physical reality. Thank the Universe for its guidance and support and then rise in your own time.

What are the advantages of meditation?

Meditation can be done anywhere and everywhere, especially if the channel is kept constantly open for immediate guidance. It is like gathering useful information prior to a trip to facilitate the journey, so that conscious choices, from the many opportunities available, can be made and life experiences made as pleasant and worthwhile as possible. The phenomenal rewards gained from the abundant wealth of cosmic information, increase personal wellbeing and encourage the spontaneous flow of creative forces. With mind, body and soul being open channels for Universal energies they are constantly revitalised, rejuvenated and re-energised.

Exercise to understand the meaning of life's situations

List all the traumatic and dreadful times in your life and choose one such event to note the subsequent sequence of happenings. Can you see a pattern emerging and a reason for the initial incident?

For example: When first qualifying as a Reflexology Therapist, I was totally disenchanted with the training, feeling it to be a waste of time and money. This is no reflection on the course itself, simply that it failed to meet my personal requirements. Becoming more of a sceptic than ever, with many doubts and questions, I researched the subject in depth. This led to the writing of four books and the

formation of an international training establishment. Today I travel extensively throughout the world holding training courses and presenting papers at International Congresses. Thousands of people are now able to enjoy this Universal wisdom and make changes for the better in their own lives. None of this would have happened had the training course met my personal requirements.

The world of dreams

What are dreams?

Dreams are a superior source of Universal intelligence, creativity and other infinite powers. Remembered or not, these visions are messages from the Higher Self that provide direction throughout life. They are one of the most powerful channels available to everyone, with extraordinary dreams often suggesting a larger intelligence at work within the mind. Some dreams are unintentional suggestions from the Conscious self to the Subconscious mind, whilst others express the suppressed fears and wishes of the dreamer. The Universe uses dreams to communicate with individual souls at a time when the conscious self is at rest in sleep.

What is experienced whilst asleep?

During sleep the body relaxes and the physical senses become muted. As the consciousness dissolves, the Subconscious takes over until the whole mind is lost in thought as massive waves of drifting, dissolving, tumbling sensations are experienced. Meanwhile the alert intuition acts as a giant perceptive ear until body, mind and soul merge with creation to resonate with all that is heard. As the body and mind dissolve into the expansive Universal realm through deep sleep, the Guardian Angel looks after each soul, to protect its pattern of individuality so that everything remains intact on waking.

WHAT HAPPENS TO THE MIND AND SOUL?

The mind and soul astral travel during sleep to visit other planes and levels of consciousness that are not bound by time or space. Many dreams are actual visits with other souls, to help those who need assistance in crossing over from the physical into the spiritual world at the time of death. Whilst asleep there is little or no awareness of a separate self, simply a state of being in a deep, dreamless sleep of pure intention and complete psychic oneness.

WHY DO WE DREAM?

Many dreams appear to come true since their nature and characteristics are determined by the content of thought when falling asleep. They are the spiritual experiences of life's reality that provide extraordinary insight into current affairs. It is possible to obtain guidance, solutions and predictions.

EXERCISE TO GAIN INSIGHT FROM DREAMS

The best way to receive advice from dreams is to focus on the issue whilst falling asleep.

Method 1 Note all your feelings about current situations and reduce them to a single phase that expresses the heart of the matter. Repeat this phase over and over again whilst falling asleep.

Method 2 Write a letter to your Higher Self and ask for assistance by outlining the situation with as much detail and information as possible. Place the letter under your pillow or next to the bed.

Can dreams assist the healing process?

For a long time dreams were valued as diagnostic and prescriptive tools but were used less to heal. It is now realised that whilst in the dream state, the body may be receptive to having its genetic code re-programmed which can allow miraculous healings to occur.

What influence have dreams had on the course of history?

Many mysterious and wondrous dreams have determined historical events and will continue to shape the future. Religious experiences include stories of how Joseph, Mary and the three wise men were alerted to the coming of Jesus, while Buddha's mother learnt of the significance of her son through a dream. Mohammed received his religious calling in the same way. Psychic, religious and inspirational dreams happen to more than just illustrious individuals of the distant past since everything is a dream of the imagination, seen in the mind's eye, long before it becomes a reality. Scientific discoveries, technological inventions, creative literature and inspirational art are all channelled through from a Divine source, whilst many musical compositions are transcribed on waking after a deep motivating sleep.

Exercise to remember dreams

Recall of dreams assists greatly in developing channelling abilities.

- Dreams occur in a particular stage of sleep during which the body is temporarily paralysed. With each movement, a part of the dream memory is erased so it is important not to change positions until the dream is fully recalled. Then roll over to recall another dream. Try various poses to see how many memories can be stirred.

- Before getting out of bed, write down every thought that comes to mind, regardless of whether it makes sense or is believed to be a dream or not. The recall process itself is easy although initially it may take time for the dream memory to appear.

Exercise in Deciphering Dreams

Everyone can learn to interpret his or her own dreams with the best interpretation being given by you. Through application, the interpretation comes of its own accord bringing the required awareness and meaning.

- Ask your Higher Self for guidance and note everything that comes to mind, imagined or otherwise. Look for clues and intuitively try to put some or all of them into practice. Initially choose something simple. For example, if there is blue in your dream add blue to your outfit that day.
- If the meaning is incomprehensible request a follow-up dream to clarify the interpretation. Meditation helps in comprehending the meaning.
- Thank the Higher Self for the guidance provided and hold on to your dream.

There is inside you all the potential to be whatever you want to be,
All the energy to do whatever you want to do.
Imagine yourself as you would like to be, doing what you want to do,
And every day take one step towards your dream.
And although at times it may seem too difficult to continue,
Hold on to your dream because one morning you will awake
To find that you are the person that you dreamed of.
Doing what you wanted to do simply because you had the courage
To believe in your potential and hold on to your dream.

10

HEIGHTENING THE SENSES

What are the senses?

The senses are highly tuned sensory instruments that continually assess the outside world to detect changes in the environment. In this way, the most appropriate response for personal development and wellbeing can be made for body, mind and soul to know how to think, feel, act and react. Every sensory experience, whether seen, heard, smelt, touched, thought or felt immediately alters the body's tone and tension levels as a form of self-protection.

How are sensations interpreted?

All incoming messages are deciphered by billions of memory cells in the brain that are linked and associated with past experiences. Undue concern, anxiety and fear cause them to overreact and become intolerant of environmental conditions. In extreme situations, this heightened irritability results in lack of endurance leading to allergies, sinus congestion and mal-absorption syndrome. Decreased sensitivity, from feeling cut off or excessively apprehensive, can result in symptoms such as numbness and paralysis. Physical affection, emotional security and spiritual awareness are essential for the maintenance of balance.

What are inner senses?

Senses that are in tune with the internal dimensions of the essence of life are subtler than those that exist on the physical plane. These fine-tuned fibres, like radar, detect indiscernible vibrations, making it possible to experience the spirit in its purist form. Tuning into these refined wavelengths assists in the development of visionary, psychic and clairvoyant skills for re-acquaintance with the inner being.

Exercise to tune into the inner senses

Pay attention to everyday details and learn from them until, eventually, it becomes a way of life. Use the following techniques to enhance the process.

- Be still in a comfortable position with your eyes closed and ask for Universal assistance to facilitate the process. Take in three long, deep breaths, hold them and as you breathe out feel all tension dissipate.
- Identify all sounds within your immediate environs and within the surrounding vicinity. Attune to each individually to determine whether there is any strain or tension. Listen for the melody of life. Sense the texture of the floor and surrounding air without touching.
- Lift your hand to gently caress the skin on your face beginning at the forehead and 'listen' to what it is saying. Touch your hair to 'see' how it is feeling. Each day, explore another part of your body and through your finger tips detect the individual needs of each cell. In your mind's eye, send bright golden, silver and white rays of light to every part and 'watch' these vibrant energies penetrate the skin and travel deep within the body.
- Without moving, open your eyes and concentrate on everyday details that are so often taken for granted. Feel their texture. Hear what they are saying. Smell their perfume. Be aware of all sound, smells and sensations, physically, intellectually, emotionally and spiritually.

- Take in another three deep breaths and thank your Spirit Guide before rising.
- Within the home and place of work, repair, throw out or replace all dysfunctional equipment. Replace worn-out light bulbs, chipped tiles, cracked mirrors, and smashed windowpanes and repaint where necessary.
- Ineffectual equipment represents parts of the body that are no longer functioning effectively, some of which have become desensitised and senseless. Once activated complete awareness is possible.
- Chips, cracks and smashed articles indicate thoughts and emotions that have been shattered. When these are sorted out, all beliefs of inadequacy, detachment or fragmentation disappear. Light bulbs illuminate situations by providing insight whilst fresh coats of paint create more room to reflect and interact.
- If you own a car, apply the same principle to facilitate personal progress through an innate mindfulness of the self.

After these exercises, most people feel refreshed, rejuvenated and alert. However, it is not unusual to feel slightly tired or experience possible aches and pains as suppressed hurts surface to be released.

WhAt is the CONNECTION BETWEEN chANNELLING AND seNsory perception?

The human intellect is bound by senses that confine it to physical and intellectual reasoning with the equilibrium being more commonly upset by the view that is taken than by what actually happens. When the more subtle dimensions are first used, one sense tends to be predominantly relied upon, with guides being heard, visions received, symbols observed, colours seen or sensations felt. However, it is best, to try and utilise all the senses to allow the body, mind and soul to become one vibratory detector. Channelling assists the process by stilling the mind, soothing over-sensitivity and creating an inner peace for clarity of vision, deeper understanding and an overall sensation of wellbeing.

Which sense is the most evocative?

Smell is the most abstract yet it influences the condition of the body, mind and soul instantly and powerfully. This is because odours are linked to personal memories and evoke emotional responses rather than intellectual recall. An environment filled with an assortment of smells, aromas and fragrances stirs an incredible variety of reactions as every smell means something different to each individual.

BEING A VISIONARY

How do thoughts and emotions affect vision?

Everything is initially seen through the mind's eye, then with the eyeballs. Once something is imagined and intuitively grasped, the eyes add the physical details which means that it is the imagination that determines the pattern of information gathered, whilst eyes add the finer details. Distressing, fearful thoughts distort these images and strain the eyes, whereas unconditional love and understanding fill these visions with a clarity that extends beyond the physical. Foresight and hindsight, therefore, are affected more by what is in the mind than what is actually seen. By clearing the mind of all perceptions it is possible to become a visionary.

Does extraordinary eyesight exist?

It is generally believed that eyes are required to differentiate between concepts within the physical world and sensations within the human body. Yet in Zen archery, separation from the target means having to learn to hit it with an arrow, whereas becoming one with the target, means that the weapon naturally returns home. Zen Masters invariably hit the bull's eye when blind folded.

What constitutes a vision?

When Martin Luther King Junior said 'I have a dream', it was in the visionary sense knowing that to make it happen all that was required was support and enthusiasm. Individuals are elected to confront national or world problems in the, often, vain hope that their vision will conjure up solutions. However, this time-honoured privilege is often corrupted through ego, pride and greed, whilst true insight is ridiculed and ignored. In time, governments will dissipate and everyone will become linked to the Divine source and personally obtain the Universal guidance and vision required.

Why are visionary concepts important?

The imagination's ability to produce amazing and extraordinary visions often upsets the status quo yet they are essential for shaping future world events. Without prophets and visionaries there would be no inventions, progress or evolution. Patterns creatively shaped within the mind stimulate self-image, essential for personal success and ongoing progress. Mental forms continually influence the body, mind and soul by either having a stimulating or depressing effect. Visualisation reinforces and strengthens the image so that when it penetrates at atomic level, behavioural patterns and personal characteristics are deeply affected. Unfortunately too many visions are lost due to lack of confidence in implementing the idea, which is a pity since activating incredible Universal concepts ensures personal success and planetary evolution.

Who are visionaries?

Everyone is a visionary since ideas first need to be visualised and then put into practice. Active visionaries clearly 'see' extraordinary future events and inventions with complete conviction long before they are perceived by others. Great faith and utmost belief may be required

before exceptional thoughts can be brought to fruition, and it is often the questioning of cynics, critics and antagonists that eventually gives validity to these concepts.

WHAT ARE THE BENEFITS?

Innovative images come to life in the form of new products and services as well as revolutionary theories and social structures. Many amazing visionary ideas have manifested as new forms of transportation, electricity, television, computers and so on throughout the twentieth century, all of which were scorned at their concept, yet today they have become so much part of everyday life that they are inevitably taken for granted. The notion that mass thought patterns and accumulated emotions can control weather patterns and earth structures is currently doubted but this Universal truth will in time, become an accepted way of thinking and ultimately prevent further 'natural' disasters. Psychics predict the future by examining energy forms and etheric patterns that are present in the imagination and are shaping the person's reality. In the ethereal realm the imagination is a channel of prediction.

WHAT EXACTLY IS VISUALISATION?

The act of visualisation involves holding the product of the imagination firmly in mind and acting as if it will materialise. The harnessing and shaping of these imaginary forces makes it possible for them to be created in physical reality. Through visionary daydreaming the imagination seeks out new, creative, patterns of possibility. With visualisation, the imagination acts as a channel allowing creation to become a fact.

EXERCISE IN OBTAINING VISIONARY GUIDANCE

Guidance can be obtained from inspirational daydreams. To heighten awareness of the process imagine your Higher Self approaching

whilst in a special place. Bask in the essence and special qualities of
this magnificent being. Express all that is on your mind and then be
still whilst listening to the responses. Trust your imagination and
become a channel of wondrous teachings and guidance.

LISTENING TO THE INNER VOICE

WHAT IS THE INNER VOICE?

The inner voice is the stirring of the deep consciousness that is directly
linked to the Universal source that provides guidance and reassurance
in everyday activities. Channelling amplifies the meaning of the small
inner voice for greater understanding to be obtained.

EXERCISE TO HEAR THE INNER VOICE

- Sit comfortably with eyes closed and ask for Universal guidance.
- Be still and centred as you begin with an arduous decision. As
  alternative solutions come to mind remain non-judgemental and
  non-critical. Take everything into consideration and allow your
  inner voice to indicate the best course of action. Then commit
  yourself to follow through with a decision. Take some deep
  breaths to physically return.
- Express gratitude for assistance received. If still not sure continue
  to the next stage.
- As above, sit comfortably with your eyes closed and request
  Universal assistance. Be as still as possible and focus on feelings
  of uncertainty. Ask if the resolution from the first stage is a good
  one. Listen within for a 'Yes' or 'No'. The intuitive response will
  be a voice, feeling or thought, with the answer being the first
  thing that comes to mind.
- Express appreciation for any direction received.

Talking in tongues

What does 'talking in tongues' mean?

When mouthpieces of a spirit communicate in ways that are not their own, they are perceived to be 'speaking in tongues'. Many channellers relay information in this way as oracles of inspiration from the Divine source.

Why do some individuals talk in their sleep?

Talking whilst asleep is the Subconscious mind trying to be heard. When others hear and relay the message, the individual is made aware of specific issues and is given a chance to think about them, even if they do not make too much sense at the time.

Opening the channels of creativity

What are channels of creativity?

Anything that gives expression to the emotions, whether through song, dance, art, music or speech, is a channel of creativity. The arts powerfully channel the inner essence, vibrancy and substance of the spirit. All that is required to be an effective channel of creativity is to express the magnificent essence of your own soul.

how can creativity be enhanced?

Creativity flourishes with improved self-esteem and self-confidence through the open expression of the true self. Everyone is naturally creative, especially when all personal expectations and any form of self-doubt are set aside. The arts are an excellent outlet and a fun way of appreciating all aesthetic aspects of life since they reflect ethereal forms. Visits to museums and galleries can provide inspiration by seeing other viewpoints through the various artists' perception.

What about those who are naturally gifted?

Everyone is naturally gifted, it is just that some are more conscious of it and actively develop their talents. Once Divine inspiration is acknowledged to be the source, the creative energy can be brought to life through the spontaneous flow of imagination. Being an open channel makes it easier to cultivate these blessings and produce magnificent works of art in a variety of forms.

Exercise that enhances creative expression

- Imagine being a seed in the dark confines of the soil and feel yourself pushing up and breaking through to appear above the surface. Experience the sudden bright light and the gentle breeze that bursts into gusts of strong wind. Be aware of different sensations and sounds throughout the day or night. Imagine absorbing water through your roots, with the moisture penetrating every cell, as nutrients, transformed by sunlight, become food for your body. Picture your cells multiplying and shaping as you change from a seedling into a fully grown plant.
- Sense ants and caterpillars crawling up your stem and butterflies, wasps and flies landing on your leaves. Rejoice at the buds opening into the most exquisite flowers and feel vibrant energy

from the sun, earth and air fill the beautiful flowers with colour and exuberance for all to enjoy.
- Wonder at the plant's ability to be such a magnificent channel of creativity and marvel at its enthusiasm and determination to grow and develop naturally within a nurturing environment. Humans are able to do the same through experiencing the extremes of emotion, the elation as well as the fears, for the harmony and rhythm to be creatively expressed.

WHAT IS ART THERAPY?

Art inspires and forms greater awareness and as a therapy it assists in the outward display of inner thoughts and feelings, especially those that cannot be verbally related. In this way, the root cause of disease can be understood and the most appropriate remedy determined.

THE RHYTHM OF LIFE

HOW CAN MUSIC ASSIST THE CHANNELLING PROCESS?

Music is a channel that excites emotions, arouses memories and generates a host of other thoughts and urges. It can elevate the senses to such sublime levels to gain an innate awareness of the Divine Spirit. Without thinking, feet and fingers often tap to the beat of music, whilst through singing, chanting and dancing the physical body can become a channel of rhythm that fills the whole with light and colour.

WHAT IS MUSIC THERAPY?

Musical rhythms and beats arouse various patterns of thought and can evoke troublesome emotions, irksome concepts and disturbed moods, which can be unconsciously expressed according to the type

of music making it easier to understand the troublesome source. Harmonious melodies change the mood bridging the gap between the physical body and the infinite reaches of the mind for an inner peace to be attained. New Age tunes are a particularly effective way of entering an altered state off consciousness.

Exercises to tune into the vibrations of sound

Singing and humming are the highest vibrations that can be achieved in the physical body which is why religious music and choral pieces can be so uplifting.

- Enjoy singing, humming or whistling and instead of mind talk try making up melodies and sounds that empathise with your thoughts and feelings, then outwardly express them. Chant various sounds ...oom...aah...mmm...ohh...yeh... to experience their vibrant effect by altering the pitches and finding ways in which to make your whole body resonate. Set aside self-consciousness and delight in the amount of feeling evoked. Hum frequently, even silently, and tunes will be channelled through to assist in spontaneous, improvised self-expression.
- Listening and tuning into inspirational music, whilst relaxing, powerfully opens the channels of creativity and visions.
- The kitchen is filled with a variety of musical instruments such as cutlery, wooden spoons, pots, pans and baking trays making it a potential musician's paradise.
- Whenever feeling afraid, uncertain or sad, whistle, sing or hum a happy tune.

Exercise that opens the channel of expression

Movement of music mobilises feelings through actions and powerfully transforms emotions. Dancing out moods creates awareness of personal values and needs.

- Choose music that makes you feel good and move freely to express your innermost feelings. Conjure up images and try to interpret these movements since they are channelled through to bring meaningful messages. Wrap your arms around yourself and waltz around the room.
- Choose Bach Flower Remedies, Australian flower or South African flower essences and absorb the qualities of one flower essence at a time by tuning in to pick up its tone. Select some music and enact the role of the flower. For example, if its essence releases childhood fears, skip and hop like a child and liberate the self.
- Join a local dancing club or form your own gathering. Through the camaraderie of others issues can be appropriately dealt with.

CAN NATURE help?

Nature's interlocking forms, splash of vibrant hues and variety of textures provide continual inspiration. Spend time listening to the sounds of nature and feel at one with your surroundings. Hear the wind in the trees, tune into the splashing of water, sing with birds, hum with bees, dance with insects, even if it is only in the mind. Enjoy discovering the many ways to harmonise with nature's sounds. Revel in the delight of experiencing this completely different dimension of life.

Nature is everywhere to reflect and inspire the human soul. Vulnerable seeds, despite the odds, still emerge to blossom and bloom serving as a reminder of the power and persistence within everyone to grow and develop creatively in everyday life.

EXERCISE THAT ASSISTS IN EXPERIENCING THE MAGIC OF NATURE

Imagine being a rosebush and allow the images to work themselves into your body. If you feel strange doing this, ask a young child to show you or just imagine the process. With feet apart mimic the position and movement of a rosebush. Converse with it and 'listen'

to what it is saying. Silently hum as the nutrients rise up through the body making 'aah', 'oou', 'eeh' sounds as you close your eyes. Spread and move your arms like branches in the breeze allowing your fingers to play with the air and sunbeams. Feel energy gushing up through the feet and body until it escapes into the surrounding atmosphere. Bow your head and imagine it to be a rosebud, and as it gradually blossoms lift your head, open your eyes and smile. Feel the humming vibration of the buzzing bee as it flits between the petals to draw nectar. Sing for joy. Join with the plant spirit. Allow your head to bow again for another rosebud to bloom. Then sit with the plant and observe its energy patterns, not with the eyes but with the whole being. Remain relaxed and allow the sensations of unseen forces, etheric intelligence or whatever to emerge.

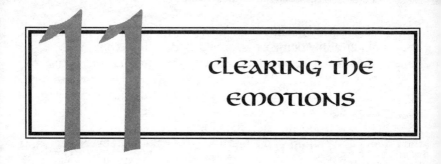

CLEARING THE EMOTIONS

What are emotions?

Emotions are energies in motion that manifest as feelings to provide sensitivity to the spirit. Active channelling brings through forms of knowing that are impossible to describe on the basis of anything that has ever been learnt, since the knowledge comes from within and is invariably accurate. Tuning into these hunches assists in the flow of the imagination and helps release many unresolved issues.

Why is there so much tragedy?

Violation is experienced in countless ways through some form of insensitivity that emerges from perceivably inexcusable actions. When these are believed to be extremely hurtful, the temptation to retaliate can be forceful. However, understanding and forgiveness, first of the self and then of others, is the greatest weapon that provides the arms to embrace. When it is hard to apologise, ask yourself 'Why?' Search within for a way to let go and break free form the destructive cycle of abuse.

> *Life is too short for grievances, for quarrels and for tears,*
> *What's the use of wasting precious days and years?*
> *If there is someone to forgive, forgive without delay,*
> *Maybe we were part responsible, so let's make up today.*
> *Be generous, forget the past and take a better view,*

Cast away the bitterness to let the sun shine through.
If it is within your power a broken heart to mend
Remember that love is all that really matters in the end!

From the depths of despair comes an incredible lightness of being which makes unbelievable heights attainable through enlightenment.

Exercise to release threatening emotions

Over a period of time, emotions kept close to the chest and contained by the breath, build up and interfere with the natural flow of life sustaining energies that hinder personal growth and development. Forgiveness and unconditional love set the soul free.

- Relax and breathe in to take in the precious life forces. As you breathe out 'get everything off the chest' by inwardly saying 'I lovingly release all anger, fear and frustration', stating specific emotions if necessary.
- With the next breath take in understanding and compassion, then let go of further emotions, this time packaged in unconditional love and wrapped in a pink cloud. Repeat as long as required until finally taking in peace and total acceptance.
- Finish by breathing out immense joy and expansive appreciation to spread love and peace throughout the Universe.
- All forms of natural healing, such as reflexology, massage, rebirthing, past-life regressions, Reiki and others assist in cleansing the body, mind and soul of old hurts, making space for healing to occur.

What is true love?

Love is a channel of miracles filled with patience, kindness, gentleness and forgiveness. This all-embracing vibration powerfully dissipates fear and reinforces faith in the Divine Spirit and the self. It contains the spark of the creative spirit that brings all souls to life. When

shared unconditionally, it transcends all concepts of cause and effect knowing that where there is life, there is hope: if there is hope, there is possibility and wherever possibility exists, love directs it better than hatred and greed. The love of money and fame are worthless without recognition of self worth and appreciation of the soul. Reaching out unconditionally to another soul automatically forms a channel of love through the extention of warmth, joy and understanding from deep within. Ultimately overall harmony will contribute to world peace. Humans were created out of love and that love should remain as a guiding light throughout life.

Exercise in loving the self

Appreciate all your talents and imagine life without any one of these assets. Look back to see how far you have come. Then decide which attributes you admire in others and look for similar qualities within yourself. 'It takes one to recognise one'.

What is the effect of love?

With every heartbeat, love is channelled throughout to cherish and nurture all cells. Whatever the heart dwells upon and how the mind thinks, influences circulation and becomes the experiences of life. When loving energies are distributed freely, mind, body and soul take on a more desirable form and can overcome insurmountable odds making seemingly impossible changes in otherwise hopeless situations.

Can channelling boost self-confidence?

Unworthiness complexes of self-doubt and low self-esteem give rise to concern about what others might think and fear of making a fool of the self, prevents the true essence from emerging. Channelling recognises that every soul, without exception, is unique and has a

meaningful and worthwhile contribution. The Creator intends the world to have your expression, so enjoy being yourself and appreciate others to balance the give and take in life.

UNDERSTANDING AND FREEING EMOTIONS

EXERCISE TO RELEASE SPECIFIC FEELINGS

Dealing with and liberating potentially detrimental sentiments prevents uneasiness and disease. Use the general descriptions and guidelines that follow to understand the underlying cause. Know that your response, no matter how intense, is ideal, so dismiss any concept of guilt and determine how best to sort out and eliminate the emotion. Although certain issues can be released immediately, others may reoccur at particular stages of personal development. For example: maths problems become increasingly challenging at various levels of education, but with increased comprehension and greater awareness, solutions are clearer and more manageable, until eventually they are no longer a threat. Likewise personal issues go through cycles of advancement for new light to be thrown on various situations to make the lessons of life more manageable and comprehensible.

- **Anger** arises from being inflamed and infuriated at having personal belief systems threatened and can be dissipated through the accepted view that many opinions contribute to an overall concept.
- **Animosity** when it is seemingly impossible to accept another requires an in-depth look at the exact reason and the improvements required. Then make changes within yourself, since others reflect personal issues that need to be dealt with.
- **Annoyance** at being uncomfortable and awkward. This can be overcome through belief in oneself.

- **Dejection** from perceived rejection, inadequacy or unacceptability necessitates approval of the self by the self.
- **Depression** occurs when lost in the dark, lacking direction or feeling without purpose. 'What on earth am I doing here?' It can ultimately lead to enlightenment, when light is thrown on the situation making it possible to lighten up and take life less seriously.
- **Despondency** from being continually disappointed from trying to please others evaporates when all thoughts, words and deeds come from the heart and soul.
- **Exasperation** at ideas not being grasped or understood requires tolerance for those who take time to think or see things rather differently.
- **Indignant** at not having received approval. Recognition however, comes from within through self-acknowledgement.
- **Infuriation** at feeling enraged at unsuitable actions or at the lack of an appropriate response. To regain composure realise that life is filled with unexpected challenges, each of which provides another exciting dimension.
- **Irritation** from extreme intolerance due to exceptionally high expectations of the self and others is soothed when everyone, including the self, is allowed to perform in their own unique way.
- **Offence** from feeling wounded and humiliated at the perceived lack of respect calls for honouring the self and others at all times.
- **Resentment** of harsh, sarcastic, caustic comments needs to be replaced with gentleness, understanding and kindness for the pleasures of life to be enjoyed.
- **Sorrow** from regret, lament, grief or mourning disappears when good ideas are immediately implemented and there is peace of mind.

Exercise to sever the emotional ties

When contact is made with another soul, no matter how briefly, a connection is made, with the intensity depending on the depth of feelings evoked. The following procedure is the most beautiful gift,

especially after a separation, divorce, retrenchment or death since both souls are given the space to be themselves. It also strengthens close relationships.

- Imagine conversing with the person concerned and regardless of feelings, make sure that both of you are smiling. Then visualise the most exquisite ribbons, each a vibrant colour of the rainbow, emerging from the energy centres to join you together.

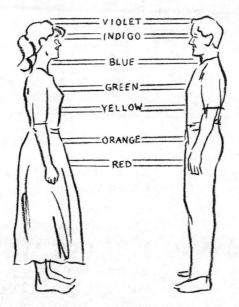

VIOLET
INDIGO
BLUE
GREEN
YELLOW
ORANGE
RED

The ribbons connecting the energy centres

- Picture the most beautiful pair of exceptionally sharp golden scissors and neatly cut, exactly half way, each ribbon in turn, beginning with the red ribbon at the bottom. As the two halves recoil, visually wrap them in separate puffs of pink cloud of unconditional love.
- Repeat with the orange ribbon then the yellow ribbon and so on, until all ties have been severed. At the end, allow a large pink cloud to tenderly immerse the other person until they are no

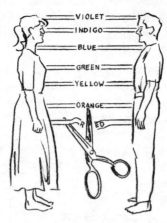

Cutting the ribbons

longer visible and then feel a pink cloud embracing you. Enjoy the inner peace that follows.

- It may to necessary to repeat the process frequently over a period of time until complete separation has been achieved.

STABILISING THE EMOTIONS

HOW ARE EMOTIONS CONTROLLED?

The endocrine system is a network of interconnected glands linked through the nervous system and blood stream, as well as through a means that science has yet to discover. Under the direction of the hypothalamus, at the base of the brain, physical, chemical, intellectual, emotional and spiritual changes are detected, which alter hormonal secretion for inner harmony and peace. It is here and not the brain, that mind and body merge, with the type of interaction between the endocrine glands being directly influenced by thoughts and emotions. These determine the amount of equanimity available for cosmic energies and Universal consciousness to inhabit the body and be present in physical awareness.

What is psychoneuroimmunology?

Attitudes and emotions immediately influence the state of immunity since the immune system acts as transducer and transforms mental energy from an active form into a more lively or languid source. Patterns of psychic and mental energy are immediately changed into physical patterns to determine the amount of resilience and vice versa. When the mind is centred on an ideal, the Kundalini energy is activated. Kundalini is an ancient Hindu word referring to the body's metaphysical energy, which is represented by the coiled snake that has become symbolic of healing in modern medicine. Originally Kundalini was the Deity of speech, the energy of which is affected and affects all thoughts and feelings. The gift of inspired speech, attributed to the Divine Spirit, is embodied as a dove to symbolise peace.

The relationship with chakras

What are chakras?

The word 'chakra' means 'wheel' and is used to describe vibrant vortexes of energy that invigorate the body and bring it to life. Seven main psychic centres, situated in the trunk and head, vibrate to certain resonances and colours that match the hues of the rainbow. Hence the origin of the word 'human being' is the 'being' or existence that 'manifests' in various 'hues'. These psychic centres are the spiritual counterparts of the endocrine glands, with each being the physical manifestation of a chakra centre. Their vibrations unify to create inner harmony and peace for body, mind and soul to become natural channels of Universal information and wisdom.

how aRe the chakRas aNd eNdocRiNe glaNds liNked?

- The pituitary gland, the master endocrine gland, and the crown chakra form the doorway to spirituality with direct access to the Higher Self and the Universe.
- The light-sensitive pineal gland and the third eye are centres of intuition and clairvoyant vision that determine natural life cycles.
- The thyroid and parathyroid glands are linked to the throat chakra to facilitate the liberal exchange of energy between the physical and metaphysical worlds.
- The thymus gland, the seat of the soul, and heart chakra fill the whole with unconditional love and acceptance of the self and others.
- The adrenal glands, connected with the solar plexus chakra, provide the courage to put thoughts into action for new ideas to be conceived.
- Female sex glands, together with the genital chakra, generate new life through the active exchange and expansion of energies for balance and equality.
- Male sex glands and the base chakra provide basic security for personal growth and development for actualisation of the soul.

Is the KuNdaliNi coNNected to the chakRas?

The semi-coiled Kundalini snake rises up and passes through the centre for each chakra to naturally infiltrate and harmonise the energy from top to bottom. Once the true spirit returns and as the centres become increasingly vibrant, a profound transition is gracefully achieved as the psychic centres become increasingly activated. The Lord's Prayer is a natural formula for balancing and opening the psychic energy centres.

7	Crown chakra	(Spirituality)	*Our father,*
6	Intuitive chakra	(Space)	*Who art in Heaven*
5	Throat chakra	(Expression and recognition)	*Hallowed be thy name*
4	Heart chakra	(Feelings of love)	*Thy kingdom come.*
3	Solar plexus	(Doing)	*Thy will be done,*
2	Genital chakra	(Communications and relations)	*On earth as in heaven.*
1	Base chakra	(Security)	*Give us this day our daily bread.*
1	Base chakra	(Mobility within society)	*And forgive us our trespasses*
2	Genital chakra	(Give and take)	*As we forgive those who have trespassed against us.*
3	Solar plexus	(Action)	*Lead us not into temptation,*
4	Heart chakra	(Love and compassion)	*But deliver us from evil.*
5	Throat chakra	(Two-way exchange)	*For Thine is the Kingdom.*
6	Intuitive chakra	(Thoughts)	*The power and the glory,*
7	Crown chakra	(Spirituality)	*For ever and ever.*
			Amen

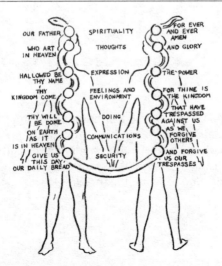

The Kundalini snake and the Lord's Prayer

99

Exercise to balance the energy centres

Sit comfortably or lie on your back with your eyes closed and ask for Universal guidance. Place both hands lightly over or just above each chakra in turn, starting with the base chakra and visualise the related colour or any other colour that comes to mind and hum. Gradually raise the tone and feel the elevated vibration energising the centre. The length of time required varies so trust your intuition.

Chakra	Position to hum	Colour	Musical note
Base	Over the crotch	Red	Middle C
Genital	Midway on the lower abdomen	Orange	D
Solar plexus	Above the belly button	Yellow	E
Heart	Over the chest	Green	F
Throat	Around the neck	Blue	G
Intuition	Between the eyebrows	Indigo	A
Spiritual	On the top of the head	Violet	B

Why is the endocrine system so important?

As the body prepares to become a conduit of spiritual awareness it needs to remain grounded for the process to occur, so that it can act as the transformational bridge between mind and matter, which is made possible through feelings. For this reason it is infinitely more effective when the emotions are balanced.

12

MAKING WAY FOR ACTION

How are individual physiques determined?

Behavioural patterns influence the development of the body's physical structure, based on protective devices that reflect many different ways of dealing with the world. For example, an overly expanded chest compensates for lack of self-esteem and self-worth, or reaches out for recognition. It caves in when feeling deflated. Hunched, raised or strained shoulders carry too many burdens or responsibilities. The physical and chemical constituents of cells respond habitually to new stimulation and experiences, whilst their memory determines the emotional response, according to whether situations are perceivably dangerous or advantageous. Constant fear and anger weaken the cells, opening them to attack, whereas joy and complete understanding strengthen their composition for enhanced resilience.

Why do reactions differ?

Unique, intricate and subtle means of emotional response develop to ensure individual survival. Many aspects are taken into account such as the personality, which is made up of many interlocking physical, emotional and mental patterns, and the body's habitual stance, formed according to perceptions and experiences of the world. Individual interpretation and assessment of the situation ultimately determine the type of reaction. Concern, anxiety and fear distort thoughts, irritate the senses and cause extreme intolerance

and irritability, which decreases the ability to deal with challenging circumstances appropriately and has an immediate impact on the physical condition of the body. Channelling opens the mind, relaxes the body and liberates the soul, creating greater flexibility throughout.

How do habits manifest?

Particular beliefs and interpretations are cultivated from personal and cultural experiences and shape the thought processes and mental patterns to determine the type of action and reaction. Perceptions of how males and females should behave are structured according to the relationship with the parents. For example, a specific experience with the father tends to embody all men with the same characteristics causing habitual responses until there is a change of mind. Reconnecting with the essence of the soul, through channelling, encourages magnificent changes and even miracles to occur on all levels.

Exercise to Loosen up

Channelling is easier when distanced from the personality and when the habitual frame of reference is relaxed. Whilst watching a favourite activity or sport empathetically become one with the performer. Feel your body moving, enjoy the freedom, sense being uplifted, taste the excitement and experience the joy. Assistance given to any one aspect of the body, mind or soul immediately effects all the other parts.

Why are there so many accidents?

Accidents bring life to a standstill, for questions to be asked and the meaning and value of individual situations to be reassessed. They usually occur when off track or when perceiving obstacles to be in the way of progress. Once back on track, channelling provides valuable clues, clear direction and meaningful information for unrestricted advancement.

Exercise to increase the quality of life

To facilitate the process, take off your watch and live each moment to the full. Realise that the gift of today is the greatest 'present' of all and with time becoming so elastic, marvel at how much more can be achieved since intuitive awareness releases the pressure. Spend time wisely and profitably to make life a worthwhile and enriching experience and, most of all, trust the flow.

The concept of energy

What is energy?

Energy is a raw potential that brings atoms to life for their physical manifestation, which is determined by their pattern of vibrations. The source is the Divine Spirit, which sends this vibrancy to earth, for everyone and everything to come to life and be part of it. Utilisation of the abundant, limitless force is determined by their enthusiastic and lively interaction, which, in turn, recharges and rejuvenates individuals. A river reproduces energy in the form of electricity, which can then activate seemingly innate objects. Energy is not ours to own since it belongs to life itself, but it is ours to use. Channel constructively and appreciatively for the benefit of all concerned.

What determines the type of energy and its utilisation?

Whether energy has a beneficial or detrimental influence depends on how it is channelled and applied since its fate, between the input and output, is shaped by the psychology of the mind and the emotions. Ideas of how to spend it and the value placed upon it determines whether a project is considered worthwhile. Meanwhile the interest

shown, the credit sought and the appreciation given regulate the incoming energy and influence the characteristics of the outgoing activity. The greater the enthusiasm, the more fulfilling the outcome. Mass energy utilisation dramatically influences the atmospheric and climatic conditions. Accumulated anger and aggression cause thunderous responses and ignites lightning reactions whilst excessive fear of being insecure results in tremors and earthquakes. Peace of mind clears the air and allows everything to settle down.

how ARE eNERGIES MANIFESTED IN human beiNGS?

Spirit is life, the mind is the builder whilst the physique is the result. There is intricate beauty in the recurrent and interlocking patterns that form the physical body and an incredible interrelationship along all life forms. Business ties, social commitments, family obligations and a thousand other duties are the soul's way of dealing with unfinished business or outstanding matters from previous lifetime experiences. New opportunities can amend the past creating space for current dreams and ambitions to be realised. Once created, all responsibilities need to be met and settled for total satisfaction and complete fulfilment on Earth. Acting responsibly means responding to the spirit and allowing the magnificence of the soul to manifest externally.

Exercises to recharge the eNERGIES

The magic of the ethereal world is often left behind in meditation or lost after inspirational workshops because it is seemly impossible to initiate spiritual concepts amidst the confusion of the physical world. Recharging the energies has a phenomenal effect in bridging the gap between the metaphysical and physical and vice versa, with exciting new concepts suddenly coming to life for no apparent logical reason. Keep the following in mind when doing the exercises:

● Whilst inhaling, the energies move upwards, in front of the body.
● During exhalation, the energies travel downwards, behind the body.

- The initiation and completion should always be in the centre, just above the navel, unless otherwise stated.

Stage 1: Restoring the vertical energies

- As you breathe in, allow the energies to rise from above the navel to the top of the head in front of the body and when breathing out, feel the vibrations move down behind the body to the base of the feet.
- With the next inhalation sense the energies once again flowing up in front of the body to the top of the head. Whilst exhaling, they follow the back of the body to return to the feet. After a couple of breaths, let the energies take off on their own. Relax and enjoy the sensation.

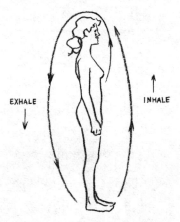

EXHALE

INHALE

The vertical energies

Stage 2: Recharging the horizontal energies

The energies now move from side to side, either from right to left or from left to right.

- Take a deep breath in and out whilst concentrating on the navel.
- On the next inhalation, imagine all the energies on the left side of the body shifting across the front of the body over to the right side, whilst on exhalation, all energies return, but this time, behind the body.

- Breathe in again allowing the energies to sweep from left to right across the front of the body.
- Keep doing this until the energies move naturally. If you wish to repeat in the opposite direction, then transfer the energies accordingly.

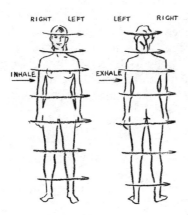

The horizontal energies from right to left. From left to right

Stage 3: Re-establishing the diagonal energies

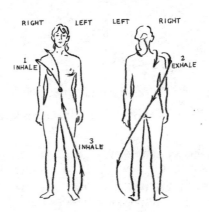

The diagonal energies from right to left. From left to right

- Inhale to raise the energies from the navel, in front of the body, to above the right shoulder. Exhale for them to cross behind the body from the right shoulder to the lower left foot. Repeat until the energies take over.
- The flow can then be along the other diagonal with the energies rising to above the left shoulder in front of the body on the inhalation and down behind the body to the lower right foot on exhalation. Again repeat or until moving alone. This transitional movement powerfully balances the masculine and feminine aspects of the soul.

Stage 4: Rejuvenating the figure-of-eight energies

- Start the energies flowing in a figure of eight, by inhaling to lift the energies in front of the body to the forehead. As you exhale the energies pass over the head, down the back of the skull, along the upper back and pass through the centre of the body, to re-emerge in front of the navel and descend to the front of the feet.
- On the next inhalation, the energies move to the back of the feet, travel up behind the legs and again transverse through the body at the navel to come up in front of the chest to the top of the head. The energies will soon start to swirl rapidly without direction.

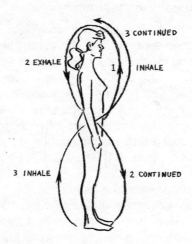

The figure-of-eight energies

Stage 5: Stimulating the spiral energies

- Although all the above energies are spiral, in this sequence they curl in a loose spiral around the body independent of the breath. From the navel they spiral upward to the top of the head and downward to the base of the feet in a very random fashion.

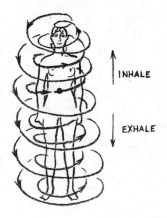

The spiral energies

Stage 6: Circulating the circular energies

- Breathe in to draw the energies into the navel area. Exhale to send them down to the right foot. When next inhaling feel them lifting and passing up along the outer edge of the right leg, through the right hip, to the centre of the pelvic area. As you breathe out sense them passing through the left hip down the outside of the left leg to the left foot and return to the right foot.
- On the following inhalation, energies whoosh from the right foot, along the outer edge of the right side of the torso, through the right shoulder to the base of the throat. Whilst exhaling the energies continue via the left shoulder, pass down the left side of the torso to the left foot before returning to the right foot.
- Next circulate the energies around the whole body.
- Three circles are formed in this way. Repeat for as long as required. The energies can then be moved in the other direction.

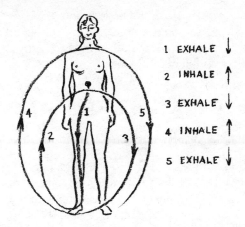

1	EXHALE	↓
2	INHALE	↑
3	EXHALE	↓
4	INHALE	↑
5	EXHALE	↓

The circular energies

Stage 7: Releasing the random energies

These energies run without direction, diagonally, vertically, spirally, or however. Set them free to do as they wish.

Note:

- Only a few minutes are required to recharge the energies, so plan to do it regularly.
- Choose a routine that suits you best, either morning, noon or night, daily or weekly, or on alternate days.
- All methods are effective whether standing, sitting or lying.

Putting creativity into action

How can creativity be actively expressed?

The written word is an ideal outlet for those with a speech defect or who lack confidence. Through creative speaking and writing,

Universal awareness can be brought into the conscious realm of thought as inspirational words are relayed from a Divine source. Wit and playfulness encourage and stimulate creativity, which is why children are so full of good ideas.

Exercise to channel information for an inspirational presentation

Meditation can be used to provide guidance, otherwise just tune in to the subject matter and allow words to present themselves in any order. Play with the meanings and sounds and focus on the feelings evoked. During the presentation, detect the spirit of the audience and allow many new ideas to come to mind, which intuitively answer their queries without being asked.

How is inspiration acquired?

Attuning to the ideals of the Higher Self opens the channel of inspiration and creativity for the spontaneous expression of the innovative. Just be yourself and do as the spirit moves you.

How can role-play and acting assist?

Taking on other characters, dressing up in costumes and using make-up, facilitates the process of channelling through the impersonation of mannerisms that are not one's own. During role-play and acting the Subconscious mind is totally absorbed into the world of the imagination, which is why hypnosis can increase the power of role playing to an incredible degree.

Being a physical outlet

How can physical abilities be developed?

To understand something better, act upon that which is already known since it is only through experience that real understanding is gained. Psychic, creative forces naturally appear and can be developed through channelling.

What causes restlessness?

Being fidgety arises from the lack of an outlet for contained energy emanating from a desire that cannot quite be acknowledged. Whilst doing one thing there is a feeling that something else needs to be done. Otherwise there is the experience of not wanting to do anything in particular but needing to do something. All this makes it impossible to sit still and relax. The stalemate of restlessness brings many possible projects to mind until one particular thought takes precedence. When activated, the uneasiness is absorbed and the energy is channelled in a more meaningful and rewarding form.

Exercise to enhance the outlet of Universal energy

Do everything with a loving and appreciative attitude. Transform work into an enjoyable, fun pastime and make recreation a time of fulfilment, rest and creation. Enjoy being a unique channel of Universal expression.

WHAT ABOUT COMPELLING NEEDS?

An intense desire is like a boomerang hurled into time with longing that comes back in the shape of fulfilment. These strong dreams, from a previous life experience, still need to be realised and attract the soul back to earth in the hope that they will now come to life. Fame, yearned for by many, can be a constructive force in the spread of the Universal message, but attachment to this glorified state makes it detrimental. To become a channel of awareness, it is necessary to emerge and create a bond with all beings and every aspect of the self.

INSIGHT INTO INSPIRATIONAL WRITING

WHAT IS INSPIRATIONAL WRITING?

Information brought through during inspirational writing is of a Divine nature and is intended to motivate, guide or direct the soul. Channelled writing is like ghost writing, in that an invisible source provides the material and directs the hand movements. At times it is a struggle to find the correct expressions, yet on other occasions the words just pour on to the page. The latter is a taste of inspirational writing. To be a constructive channel it is important to trust the process, be spontaneous and go with the flow. Attune to an ideal for mind, body and soul to resonate with the spiritual energy of creation.

IS BEING RIGHT- OR LEFT-HANDED SIGNIFICANT?

The right side of the body represents the past and the left side is symbolic of the present. Right-handed souls direct energies towards handling former issues in a creative manner whilst left-handed

people deal with the present and future in more analytical ways. Many left-handed people write with the hand turned back on itself in an attempt to come back into the present. Being ambidextrous is ideal for all aspects of life to be handled equally and is possible when using a keyboard, playing the piano and so on.

Ꭰow can the concept be understood more easily?

Handwriting is generally controlled and manipulated, requiring attention and sometimes effort. Breathing, on the other hand, proceeds unconsciously and automatically unless consciously determined. Whilst writing inspirationally, the writer has no control over hand movements, which is why the outcome can vary considerably from the person's ordinary penmanship. A state of calm detachment encourages this inspirational flow.

Exercise to achieve inspirational writing

Allow yourself to be guided as you write a short story about one or more of the following. 'The day the sun decided not to shine', 'The flight of the bumble bee', 'The story of a match stick from beginning to end'. Relax and trust the spontaneity of the writing process. If the outcome is truly remarkable and exceeds all personal concepts or current knowledge then channelling is taking place. Meditation enhances the process by ensuring that the mind, body and soul are in their most receptive state.

What will others think?

Non-acceptance arises from the disbelief that everyone possesses these extraordinary gifts. Rather than being deterred, be an inspirational example. Even if one's own life is a shambles, it is still

possible to channel profound Universal material, the interpretation of which changes as greater peace and understanding emerge.

Why is the ideal important?

In inspirational writing the Subconscious and Conscious minds work together as a channel for the Super Conscious mind. The ideal serves as a magnet and acts as a filter to determine the nature of the channelled information.

Can anything interfere with the process?

Self-consciousness, concern about doing something wrong and the need to write something important can get in the way. Avoid evaluating, censoring or filtering the words, instead allow the inspiration to flow through unhindered. Concentrate less on the mechanics and stay in touch with the spirit of the ideal. Remember that there is no right or wrong. Start by writing anything and nothing in particular.

What can be done to assist the process?

Once the writing begins, the wisdom comes, whilst a genuine need to know stimulates the output. Meditation and attunement to an ideal sharpen the flow until, in time, the writing becomes less contrived and more inspired. Eventually each word is written without having to plan it in advance. A good session is when you write freely, not when you write well. The opportunity to apply channelled material helps make sense of it. Use a thesaurus to match words with emotions and refer regularly to the dictionary to gain deeper insight.

Exercise: The daily to do List

- Appreciate the gift of life to the full and be filled with gratitude for the bounty of everyday presents. Cherish each moment as if it were your last.
- Commit yourself to your school, job and mission in life. Feel honoured that you have been entrusted with so much and make your job your hobby. Assist others but do not do everything for them. Rather provide them with the insight, skills and then, possibly, the means.
- Do it now and do it well. Leave no space for regrets or guilt. Accomplish everything to the best of your ability. Willingly try new concepts. Put at least one fresh idea into practice every day. Stick your neck out and be a pioneer.
- Make time for yourself and take pride in your appearance. Be grateful for advice, listen to 'criticism' and see things from every point of view. Always look for ways to improve and have plenty of ideas.
- Dream and visualise. Add to the list of hopes and aspirations and keep adding to it. Always carry a notepad and writing implements to note all ideas as they spring to mind. Make life an interesting and worthwhile adventure for the body, mind and soul.

13

STRENGTHENING THE CHANNELS OF COMMUNICATION

Why is interaction important?

Great pleasure can be derived from interaction whilst intuitive connection with the Universe empowers the true spirit. Everyone is intimately connected with Divine intelligence and once complete enlightenment has been attained, differences will evaporate and all souls will communicate through the common Universal language of unconditional love and acceptance.

What is required to open the channels of communication?

Unique concepts are essential for enrichment and awareness since all souls reflect one another. As each soul understands his or her unique position in relation to others, complete manifestation of its individuality in its purest form, makes it an open channel of communication and automatically links it with the Divine source making it possible to relate on any level.

Where does abusive behaviour stem from?

Violent acts occur when individuals lose control because others ignore them. Those that inflict intense pain, discomfort and misery

are so desperately unhappy, frustrated and disillusioned that all caution is thrown to the wind in a desperate attempt to obtain a reaction, no matter how drastic. The use of insulting words, hateful emotions, condemnation of others and lack of respect are all atrocious acts. It is criminal to rob the self and others of dignity or opportunities. High rates of crime arise from not fully appreciating the gift of life and the privileges that go with it. The ability to forgive the self makes it easier to forgive others and, in so doing, the vicious cycle can end.

Who is the victim?

Individuals are magnetically drawn towards one another to share experiences, talents, attributes and knowledge, as well as to learn how to deal with the favourable and adverse facets of being human. Each soul acts as a mirror to reflect the saint and the sinner, the lover and the destroyer, the pure and the corrupt, the pacifier and the tormentor that are within everyone. Pent-up thoughts and distressed emotions need a creative outlet, that can be assisted through channelling, reflexology and massage, all of which encourage the constructive flow of life-force energy. Respect for all souls and appreciation of life, make it difficult to harm or deny any other living form. Channelling and communication with Universal Guides further enhance the process.

Why is communication on every level so important?

Criticism of others stems from dissatisfaction with the self, whilst unhappiness with personal circumstances causes varying degrees of upset and trauma. Others reflect ways in which to deal with these awkward situations, yet they are generally resented for interfering. It is so easy to take the pleasures of fellowship for granted, until it no longer exists. The presence of other souls provides companionship and appreciation of hidden values within ordinary moments that

might otherwise be disregarded or lost. Harmony amongst all souls soothes the transition into a new era and ensures that everyone will safely enter the next exciting dimension of human reality for the ongoing development and enhancement of all beings.

Exercise to strengthen relationships

- Make time for special and intimate occasions. Write notes of love and appreciation with a flower or chocolate attached. From time to time give small gifts of affection instead of waiting for significant dates. Arrange to spend time with those who are particularly special in your life. Remember to say 'I love you'.
- Channelling in a group is an excellent way of uniting souls on every level. Exclusive focus on the self is set aside for harmonious action towards a common goal through the formation of a circle, the joining of hands, closing the eyes and, with soft music in the background, being still. As everyone emits sounds that make them feel good, they can then try the 'aahs', the 'eeeys', 'ays', 'oooohs' and 'yehs' together. The variety of tones allows the whole body to vibrate and resonate with joy.

Although many find this a joyful and rejuvenating experience, each individual reacts differently. Some may cry, whilst others may feel a tingling sensation. Whatever happens, it is ideal for that person and helps to open the channels of communication.

Exercise: The daily friendship list

Give hugs to open the channel of love. Every time words of criticism and condemnation reach the lips change them to words of understanding and encouragement. Take time to listen. Reach out a helping hand. Think of ways that will make the lives of others worthwhile, enriching and fulfilling. Always remember the value of a smile.

A smile costs nothing, but it means so much,
It enriches those who receive it, without impoverishing those who give it.
It happens in a flash, but its memory can last forever.
None are so rich that they can go along without it,
And none so poor but are richer for the benefits.
It is rest to the weary, daylight to the discouraged, sunshine to the sad,
And nature's best antidote in times of trouble.
Yet it cannot be bought, borrowed or stolen,
For it is something that is no earthly use to anyone, unless given away.
And if, in the rush of business, someone is too tired to give you a smile,
Then leave one of yours for no one needs a smile as much
As those who have none to give!

14

ESTABLISHING A SECURE BASE TO CHANNEL

Why is there so much insecurity?

Everything in life is an expression or channel of who and what we are. The lives we live, the possessions around us, the circumstances of our realities and all its details were once a pattern held in the mind that was channelled through as a life energy force, to physically manifest on the terrestrial plane. Insecurity arises from living an artificial, false existence, compounded by an overwhelming obsession with material wealth and intellectual prowess. So much is taken for granted, leaving little or no room for appreciation of the very essence of life. This has impoverished the intuitive, emotional and spiritual aspects of life creating widespread insecurity and fear. Security with the self and reconnection with the spirit positively affects how we experience all of life's events.

Exercise to form basic security

- Appreciate all the little things, as well as the big things and everything in between.
- Value all possessions, physically, intellectually, emotionally and spiritually.
- Cherish those people and things that are precious. Give credit to yourself and others at all times. Make all situations and actions worthwhile and fruitful.
- Spend and invest time beneficially. Enjoy enriching the mind, body and soul. Accumulate a wealth of information and

experiences. Treasure the multitude of opportunities that come your way. Share Universal wisdom for abundance on all levels.

- In the Universe, there is plenty for everyone's need, but not for everyone's greed. Infinite resources at every level of mind, body and soul are the ultimate forms of enrichment.

What does grounding the physical body mean?

Human beings house a subtle energy body that has its own network of invisible channels and sensory detectors, parallel to the circulatory system and the five senses. Whenever channelling or using other psychic abilities, the subtle body can resonate to the energies of another soul and receive impressions through the inner senses. In order to do this effectively there needs to be a conscious, stable connection between the physical and the subtle body, to keep the feet on the ground whilst the head is up in the air.

Does Heaven exist on Earth?

The home, in its true sense is a heavenly place. It is where the heart is, the place to return to after a long journey or at the end of a challenging day and where individuals can really be themselves. Making the home like Heaven on Earth is the ultimate experience.

Why is sexual energy important in establishing a secure base?

Sexuality is the strongest physical potential within the body and can have a creative or detrimental effect, depending on the focus, level of understanding and awareness of each individual. No sex act or sexual relationship is good or bad in itself, since it is the purpose or the desire for the sexual event that determines its value. If used for self-gratification only, it becomes a destructive and confusing energy

that can lead to an insatiable appetite rather than being a union of Universal oneness. Sexual energy is one of the most beautiful and intimate expressions of life and is the closest that humans can be to becoming creators themselves.

What considerations are required when channelling through new life?

One of the most cherished experiences of being a channel is that of being a parent. The birth of a child is a marvellous event and, even though the facts are fairly well understood it still remains a miracle. Conscious parenting, in which both parents take an active and responsible role, requires physical, mental, emotional and spiritual preparation prior to conception, for both to be receptive channels, whilst meditation and having fun together sharpens the focus. Since like attracts like, the parents love, mental and spiritual states and degree of consciousness attract a similar-minded soul, whereas the gender is determined by the relationship of the male/female energies at the time of conception. For example, a dominant or too weak a female energy results in the inception of a boy and vice versa. Nature balances the male/female ratio to encourage equality.

What is the influence of childhood experiences?

Memories of being a child vary considerably and there is an inner child within everyone; a living, breathing, feeling consciousness. If love was craved and never received, the disillusioned youngster appears periodically throughout life using past circumstances to extract sympathy, to avoid certain situations or to blame. This results in an existence of mediocrity, caught between childhood longings and adult deprivation, yet both the past and the future are subject to desires and decisions which can be changed at any time. Initially, this may appear impossible because the past seems so real and the

future just a dream, but life is an illusion of perceptions that can be altered at any time to create a more wholesome and enjoyable reality.

EXERCISE TO CREATE A MORE WORTHWHILE EXISTENCE

- Visualise yourself as a child, on a stage, with the backdrop of your past. Look for things perceivably lacking and detect missed opportunities filled with regret.
- Then bring yourself into the present, on to a more elaborate and sophisticated stage. Midway through an act, the distraught little child appears, demanding attention or pleading to be included, which makes progress impossible.
- Recall times that you felt disadvantaged because of some form of deprivation, abuse or neglect in your past. Do you hold your parents responsible? Are you blaming them for not supplying sufficient love and attention? See within each parent his or her own dissatisfied inner child longing for what might have been.
- Feel how desperately your little child hangs on but is unable to keep up due to lack of experience. Detect your reluctance to let go since there would be no one to hide behind or blame. Consider how much you are clinging on to a past that is of no use.
- Release yourself from this restrictive situation by giving the little child all that it needs, which can be done through the imagination or in meditation in the following way.
- Arrange to meet the little child, in you mind, at least once a week in a safe place where you are both happy, be it in a castle, in the woods, on a beach or in a tree house. Find yourself in the space first and then allow the youngster to join you. Embrace and comfort one another. Give the child anything and everything it wants. Let the child reunite you with your spark of innocence, curiosity and wonder, and allow your cynicism to be overwhelmed by hope. Offer to be your child's future and to be whatever it would like you to be when it grows up. Then start bringing these childhood dreams into your reality.

15 CHANNELLING IN THE FUTURE

Why is channelling a necessity?

The time has come to re-evaluate the true meaning of power. There has been too much suffering, denial and destruction from the use of force in the struggle for power in the world. The only way in which all souls can live peacefully together on Earth is through self-empowerment and then the world can be the friendly, wonderful place that it really is. Although seemingly impossible, this amazing concept is completely attainable since power and responsibility are linked. To gain power means taking responsibility by responding naturally to the soul and actively manifesting its true essence in its purest form. The more responsibility taken, the more powerful an individual becomes. For this to be brought into reality, assistance and guidance are required from a Divine source which, through channelling makes the endless resources of Universal wisdom abundantly available.

What are the prospects for channelling?

Channelling will ultimately become a way of life and an integral part of our perception. Children already know this and many already value and utilise these abilities within themselves. The time is perfect for individuals to tune into non-physical sources of creativity and inspiration through channelling and claim their birthright, but

the choice to utilise it will always remain with the individual. This mobile tool can be used anywhere, any time and in any way. It requires no maintenance, no spare parts, no check-ups, no fuel, no insurance and furthermore, it costs absolutely nothing. All that is required is to be an open channel and put Universal concepts into practice. It can be done anywhere, at any time, by anyone. The most important aspect of channelling is its respectful use for the benefit of all concerned.

They said to build a better world, I said I would, but how?
The world is a cold, depressing place and complicated right now,
And I'm so small, and helpless too, there really is nothing that I can do,
They said, 'Oh yes, indeed there is, just build a better you'.

AN OVERVIEW AND GUIDE TO EFFECTIVE CHANNELLING

SUMMARY OF WAYS TO CHANNEL

- Meditation channels through the meaning and essence of life.
- Imagination sets the mind free and opens it to endless possibilities.
- Creative arts for attunement to the Super Conscious realm give a glimpse of the wealth of cosmic forces.
- Unconditional love opens all channels to the greatest vibrations.
- Inspirational writing physically expresses Universal wisdom.
- Just being the self.

PRACTICAL METHODS OF FACILITATING THE PROCESS

There are seven main physical channels of energy:

1 An intuitive channel provides a direct link between the intellect and the Universe.
2 Internal and external sensory channels detect terrestrial and extra-terrestrial conditions.
3 The creative channel facilitates the two-way expression between the ethereal and physical realms.

4 An emotional channel creates space for the appreciation of the spirit through unconditional love.

5 The physical channel which beneficially activates ideas and concepts for human progress and advancement.

6 The communication channel forms pleasurable and beneficial relationships creating a greater understanding of the self through others.

7 The earth channel stabilises and energises for greater stability to generate an appreciation of the endless natural resources available.

To enhance the receptivity of each, use the following information for greater awareness of all life-energy forces. Consciously use colours to effectively alter physical vibrations and the characteristics of the energy passing through in the following ways:

- The choice of drink and food: pure water, symbolic of the spirit, facilitates the flow between the physical and metaphysical aspects of life; purple, found in beetroot, expands the mind, whilst the presence of red provides basic security for ideas to be put into action.

- The selection of clothing and accessories: as light waves filter through material, the vibrancy of its coloured hue is absorbed before penetrating the transparent skin. The tone is then set for future events.

- Decoration within the home and the layout in the garden: yellow activates and enhances intellectual pursuits; green reassures and provides space to be the self; blue soothes and facilitates expression, and so on.

- The decision as to the type of car: red, easily noticed, is great for energy and accelerates progress; silver brings the spark back into life with new reflective qualities; sports cars speed ahead; four-by-fours facilitate the more arduous routes taken.

- The décor within the place of work, be it in a office, study or school: dark, rich colours assist in deep, enriching research; light, bright colours provide light relief to brighten ideas.

Connecting with the channel of wisdom

Colour	White for the purity of spirit and indigo/violet to raise the level of consciousness and assist in connecting with ethereal energies.
Element	Ether provides space to think in unison and brings together many different aspects of the Universe.

Exercises that open the channel of thought, intuition and spiritual awareness

• Write down fears, anxieties and burdens	To recognise and release all obstacles for the restoration of faith to connect with the spirit.
• Clear the conscience	Acknowledge and understand the influence and necessity of all past concepts so that a weight is taken off the mind making it more receptive to Universal reassurance and inspiration.
• Stretch the toes	Expands the mind beyond self-imposed limitations and extends the imagination beyond the physical into the spiritual realm.
• Ask questions with the one hand and reply with the other	To access the Higher Self through the inner child for past issues to be resolved and progress to be made.
• Record dreams	Through their interpretation, vital clues are provided as to the state of the Subconscious mind and its relationship with cosmic energies.

•	Put together a wish list	Provides direction when channelling so that aspirations can become a reality.
•	See every point of view	Extends vision to appreciate that everything in life, from the most minuscule molecule to the greatest planet, is important and has a vital role to play.
•	Listen to soothing music	Inner tranquillity harmonises the finely tuned body fibres and facilitates the attunement to the vibrations of Universal wisdom and guidance.
•	Tune into the sounds of nature	Connects individuals with natural Universal cycles for the rhythmic flow of life.
•	Sketch an olfactory map by drawing all smells detected	Alerts the sense of smell so that the soul is put back on track for complete fulfilment on Earth.

OPENING THE CHANNELS OF EXPRESSION

Colour	Blue soothes and facilitates the two-way exchange and flow of vital life-force energies.
Element	Air/ether facilitate the exchange of creative energies.
Suggestions	Periodically go outside and lie on your back to look up at the sky and observe the continuous movements and shapes of the magnificent clouds. Use blue to enhance and soothe all forms of expression.
Meaning	Inspirational growth through the liberal and fair exchange of all life-force energies.

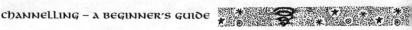

Exercises that open the avenues of expression

• Art and music	Provide outlets for creative talent.
• Beat a drum or cooking pot	Releases contained feelings and emotions.
• Enjoy aromatherapy baths	To clear all channels and arouse the sensual aspects of the self.
• Speak up for yourself	To acknowledge your individuality so that you can be true to yourself and others.

Expanding the distribution of unconditional love

Colour	Green facilitates unconditional love and complete acceptance of yourself and others.
Element	Air extends the soul and accommodates inflated feelings of self-esteem and self-worth with space to feel free.
Suggestions	Spend time with nature, enjoy open spaces, breathe in the fullness of life, love yourself and others unconditionally. Smile often and lighten up, appreciate the gift of life, place the souls of feet together to connect at soul level, enjoy green vegetables and fruits, hug trees to absorb Universal energies when feeling drained, spread your arms, throw back your head to take in large breaths of life with love and appreciation, wear green and turquoise to create space for yourself. Just be.
Meaning	Space, self-esteem, self-worth, feelings, emotions, inspiration, expansion, mobility and exchange.

Exercises that create emotional and inner harmony

• Deep breathing	Releases potentially disruptive feelings that have been kept close to the chest.
• Massage the body	Touch re-acquaints individuals with innermost feelings and the unacknowledged aspects of the self.
• The magic of candlelight	Softens and calms the atmosphere.
• Memory lane game	To understand the pattern of life, look back to see the effect of recurrent cycles to determine appropriate changes as required.
• Place a hand over each chakra and hum (see Chapter 11)	Harmonises the hormones for homeostasis.

Functioning effectively and efficiently

Colour	Yellow increases understanding by putting thoughts into action for further knowledge to be attained.
Element	Fire provides the energy and enthusiasm to activate concepts and recharge the batteries.
Suggestions	As soon as a good idea comes to mind put it into practice and, whilst on to a good thing, fire yourself with enthusiasm because a quitter never wins and a winner never quits. Wear sunshine yellow to conceptualise Universal concepts and brighten the world.
Meaning	Accomplishments, achievements, challenges and opportunities.

EXERCISES THAT ENERGISE THE CHANNELS OF ACTUALISATION

•	Recharge the energies	For the manifestation and appreciation of the physical manifestation of spiritual concepts.
•	Fast and spring-clean	For purification of mind, body and soul.
•	List all personal achievements	To appreciate those accomplishments and ambitions already realised.

ENHANCING COMMUNICATIONS AND RELATIONSHIPS

Colour	Orange brings joy through the pleasure of sharing.
Element	Water is the medium of communication that eases the flow.
Suggestions	Wear orange to lift the soul and enhance communications, drink fresh orange juice daily, introduce orange in to the home, enjoy being in your own company as well as the companionship of others and take on those aspects of life that benefit all concerned.
Meaning	Joy, pleasure, respect, conveyance, reaching out, looking within, information, correspondence, conversation, connecting.

EXERCISES THAT STRENGTHEN THE LINES OF COMMUNICATION AND RELATIONSHIPS

- Cut the chakra ties — To create space for the self and others.
- Relaxation — For physical relief through the release of tension.
- Meditation — For clarity in all relationships.

CREATING A SECURE BASE

Colour	Red stabilises, energises and grounds.
Element	Earth is saturated with mineral wealth and abundant resources, whilst its solidity provides a firm base from which to grow and develop.
Suggestions	Eat red apples, red plums, tomatoes and so on for substantial energy. Wear red to feel better about who and what you are, appreciate everything that you have in life, value your role and contribute to society. Be grateful for your home, family and health.
Meaning	Interest, appreciation, value, investment, worth, importance, significance, assets and resources.

Exercises that provide basic security

• Keep the car full of petrol/gas	Reserves of energy affording extra security.
• Appreciation list	Realise and cherish the value of your family, friends, health, parents, job, home, country, talents and the many other gifts that are too numerous to mention.
• Natural therapies such as reflexology, aromatherapy, Reiki	Reconnect body, mind and soul through the elevation of consciousness for the fine-tuned body to act as a perfect channel for the mainfestation of Universal wisdom on the earth plane for evolutionary advancement.

FURTHER READING AND RESOURCES

Books

There are so many fantastic publications available that it is almost impossible to make suggestions. It is best to visit book stores, especially those that stock more self-actualisation and esoteric material and choose for yourself. Here are some possibilities:

Behaving as if the God in all Life Mattered: A New Age Ecology, Machaelle Small Wright
Celestine Prophecies, James Redfield
Don't fall off the Mountain, Shirley Maclaine
Driving your own Karma, Swarmi Beyondananda
Going within, Shirley Maclaine
Interview with an Oracle, Ira Progoff
Many voices: The Autobiography of a Medium, Eileen Garrett
New Cells, New Bodies, NEW LIFE, Virginia Essene (Ed.)
Seeing with the Mind's Eye, Dr Mike Samuel
Soul Psychology – Keys to Ascension, Joshua David Stone
The Complete Ascension Manual, Joshua David Stone
The Laws of Psychic Phenomena, Thomas J Hudson
The Possible Human, Jean Houston
The Psychic Realm: What can you believe?, J Gaither Pratt
Traveller in Inner Space, Carol Bush

Recommended journal

Sedona Journal of Emergence, P O Box 722, Spring Hill, Brisbane 4000, Queensland, Australia. Telephone: 61 (0) 7 3399 1333

New Age Journal
7 Old Bailey Street
Central Hong Kong
Telephone: 852 8100 1939
Fax: 852 2982 4013

Free Spirit
300 San Juan Avenue
Venice
California 90291
USA
Telephone: (0)1 91 310 581 6166
Fax: (0)1 91 310 581 1186

Odyssey
The Wellstead
1 Wellington Avenue
Wynberg
Cape 7800
Republic of South Africa
Telephone: 27 (0)21 797 8982
Fax: 27 (0)21 762 7823

Nara (Western Australia's Holistic
Journal)
2/2 Glyde Street
East Freemantle
WA 6158

Audio and video tapes

There are many to choose from, so decide for yourself which appeal to you most, and listen to recordings channelled through by intangible entities such as Lazarus, Omni and so on.

Useful addresses

The ARE (the Association for Research and Enlightenment) is a non-profit, open-membership organisation committed to spiritual growth, holistic healing, etc. P O Box 595, Virginia Beach, VA 23451, USA. 67th Street and Atlantic Avenue, Virginia Beach, VA 23451, USA

Academy of Universal Healing
P O Box 1280
Rivonia 2128
Gauteng
Republic of South Africa
Telephone: 27 (0) 11 803 1552 Facsimile: 27 (0) 11 803 5946

Blair Styra (channels Tabaash)
P O Box 1156
Wellington
New Zealand
Telephone: 64 (0) 4 384 3489

Ka Huna Institute of Bodywork and Personal Development
P O Box 118
Boondall
Queensland 4034
Australia
Telephone/facsimile: 61 (0) 7 3265 1600

Light source
3134 E. McKellips Road # 211
Mesa
AZ 85213
USA
Telephone: (0)1 602 832 7633 Facsimile: (0) 1 602 832 0262

Orin and DaBen
P O Box 1310
Medford
Oregon 9750
USA

Osiriis Centre
18 Bannister Street
Freemantle
Western Australia
Telephone/facsimile: 61 (0) 314 7800

Soham Sanctuary
P O Box 16588
Atlasville
Gauteng
Republic of South Africa
Telephone: 27 (0) 11 395 1749